Walking with Ghosts

True Encounters of the Paranormal

Lisa Yorio

ISBN: 1451579632
ISBN-13: 9781451579635
Library of Congress Control Number: 2010904611

This book is dedicated in loving memory to:
My Mother – Edna Yorio –
One of the spirits that guide me through lifes
uncertain sea

TABLE OF CONTENTS

WHAT IS A GHOST?

Ghosts, what are they? Are they a figment of our imagination or are they a manifestation of our former selves? Here is a little insight on how they inhabit our world.

Many people believe a ghost or a spirit can be several things. Usually, it can be a person or many who have died suddenly in some tragic or violent way. This could be a murder, suicide, accident, or perhaps even a causality of war. On the other hand, sometimes a person may pass away from natural causes, but remain earthbound. The law of conservation of energy states that "energy can neither be created or destroyed." If this is true, when people die, their energy should still be present and active. People, who die a normal death, typically don't experience agony and are able to readily pass onto the next state of consciousness or spirit world. However, the people who die a tragic or violent death remain earthbound and are referred to as ghosts.

There are three kinds of ghosts that cause hauntings. The first can be a friend or family member who has died but has some unfinished business to attend to before they cross over to the next plane. They may want to deliver a message to a loved one to let them know they are ok, or may simply comfort them in their time of grief. This could be a relative, parent, child or friend. They may look solid and human just like we do. These sprits will not cause harm to anyone who crosses their path. They are sometimes considered to be like a guardian watching over someone. They have a strong emotional attachment to the loved ones that they left behind.

Another type of haunting is called a residual haunting. This may be a ghost or several ghosts repeating the same actions that happened at the time of their death. These spirits remain earthbound because they are unaware of what has happened to them, and that they have died. They keep acting out the same scene over and over again. Usually, they don't contact anyone. They just appear as if they were still living; unaware of their surroundings. This type of haunting is said to happen quite often on the fields of Gettysburg, Pennsylvania. There are many eyewitness accounts of soldiers marching in unison, preparing for battle, and then slowly disappearing; only to reappear and start the cycle again and again.

The third type of haunting is usually a poltergeist or an entity. These spirits are usually evil and may want to cause harm to someone. They may be attached to where they lived, the occupation they held, or someone. They may not want to leave their house for example, and anyone who moves in may cause a threat to them. Therefore, the poltergeist may rattle chains, moan, cause knocking or unusual sounds, move objects around or break things. Basically anything they possibly can do in order to scare the inhabitants of the house. This type of spirit is not always evil. Sometimes the poltergeist is a nuisance ghost, only wanting to play or make contact. This may be a child who has died some tragic way and doesn't realize it. It may bounce objects, laugh, or possibly be a prankster. This type of ghost doesn't mean any harm but just wants to make its presence known. An entity, on the other hand may be evil or demonic wanting to take possession of a person for its own gain. There really isn't any explanation why these hauntings happen. But for centuries, there have been many documented cases of this phenomenon.

There have been many recent cases of poltergeist activity that are affiliated with not a ghost but the actual person who is being haunted. They may be causing this build up of energy, which is misinterpreted as a poltergeist, when it is actually the person causing this extreme activity. Sometimes a person may be going through some emotional turmoil and they release their pent up energy in the air which causes objects to move, similar to telekinesis, which is the ability to move objects with your mind. They may sense things that are really not there. A lot of poltergeist cases, involve teenagers, who are going through adolescence. Sometimes adults can also experience this type of haunting, for instance, a woman going through menopause. She may be experiencing emotional upheaval, and channel her energy causing poltergeist activity.

Ghosts exist in their own realm. A ghost can phase in and out of a location. They can come and go as they please without a specific purpose. Some hauntings can be daily, weekly, or once every few years. There is no pattern for a ghosts existence. Many ghosts haunt places where they have lived or perhaps where they have died. They are attached to their homes or places that they have loved spending their lives, such as vacation areas. One very popular haunted area is Cape May, New Jersey. I have vacationed there myself many times.

One theory that I have discovered during my research, claims that there are different kinds of ghosts. One in particular is called a "traveling ghost". It can move distances by willing its energy around. This means they can look at something and will themselves to it by transporting themselves from one place to another. This is what most ghosts do. Some ghosts walk around but only for short distances. They remain haunting only one area. However, other ghosts move around quite a bit. This can explain why a spirit may die somewhere else but return to a different location that they loved while they were alive. The ghost plane is a realm different from ours, but it is not as advanced as the "other side". The "other side" is the next higher plane that the majority of spirits cross over to. Once this happens the spirit can no longer make contact with living. They are in a better place and watch over us and perhaps even guide us through our lives. Most ghosts like where they are, that's why they stay earthbound. They have more freedom then when they were alive. Ghosts can interact with each other, socialize and even exist as if they are alive.

Ghosts are all around us. They are everywhere. They can appear anywhere at anytime whether it be in a house, building, inn, hotel, hospital, jail, or cemetery. Ghosts feed off energy in order to appear. This is why there is a high concentration of hauntings on stairways. This is a place where most people expend alot of their energy by walking up and down the stairs. Renovations on houses or buildings also stir up alot of paranormal activity. It could be because the spirit's energy sat docile for so long and now it's being exposed or it simply doesn't like the changes being made. It may feel threatened by this. Spiritualists believe that we all have some type of ability to contacts spirits but many of us either don't know how or choose not to.

I have the ability to detect the presence of a ghost. Usually, when I sense this, I start taking pictures. I am very intuitive. I can't see or hear ghosts but I can sense that they are there.

I have caught on film, over the past few years what I believe to be anomalies caused by paranormal activity. I have compiled these over a span of seven years. These were taken on many ghost tours that I have attended throughout these years. They extend from the east coast all the way to the Southwest, where I currently reside. I have gotten the most activity in Gettysburg, Pennsylvania and Salem, Massachusetts.

In all the photographs of these haunted places there are similar lines, colors, and flashes of light. These have been sometimes known to be called tracers, or vortexes. This may look like a thick rope or a small tornado. In my pictures, they look like broken lines. They show up in various colors. I think they are a bunch of orbs moving together. An orb is a collection of energy which usually is affiliated with paranormal activity. This however, is harder to prove as paranormal since in most cases an orb
can be nothing more than a speck of dust. Another view is that these lines may be an opening into another dimension or world. The vortex is the actual portal where good as well as evil spirits may be able to cross over into our dimension.

Ghost hunters consider orbs, ectoplasm, paranormal mist, and vortexes in their opinion, evidence of spirit activity. I have been able to photograph all of these anomalies.

The collection of pictures I have are somewhat harder to debunk, even for the most critical skeptics. They have alot more detail and color then most paranormal photos. It is harder to dismiss these because they are in focus and very clear. It looks as if something is moving in front of the camera. All of these were taken on clear nights. There wasn't any rain, fog, or mist to taint these photographs.

I also usually bring someone along with me as an eye-witness to the current weather conditions, and to verify that I am only shooting into darkness. The camera can capture movement on film, that the naked eye cannot. So I don't see any of these images when I am taking these pictures. These images only appear when the film has been developed.

Ghosts can manifest in many ways. Usually on film, this can be captured in the form of mists, orbs or anomalies. These lines, that I have photographed, I believe are forms of energy from a spirit trying to manifest itself. Ghosts need to draw energy off of things such as cameras, tape recorders, lights and batteries. The battery on my camera as well as my friend's; got drained the night we where taking pictures in the Howard Street Cemetery and the Old Burying Point in Salem, Massachusetts. Sometimes, the energy can be trapped inside something physical, like a
rock, gun, or sword. This scenario is possible with some of the artifacts that were recovered on the fields of Gettysburg. These objects have remained there since the war. This is perhaps how some of the ghosts in Gettysburg are able to appear even in broad daylight as well as pitch dark.

Some people experience the paranormal, and others do not. We are all born with natural differences in perception, psychic abilities, or even just sensitivity to psychic occurrences. Some people are born with a more astute sensitivity to the paranormal. For instance, one person may smell pipe tobacco burning followed by seeing an apparition of a ghost while the other person standing next to them does not. This means one person is more sensitive to the paranormal then the other. Experts believe such an individual can develop their own psychic abilities. I believe I am sensitive to the paranormal. On July 5, 2006 I revisited Gettysburg for the third time. Although I didn't get much activity in the photos compared to the previous year, I did encounter something strange. As I was walking down the street, I smelled gunpowder, but a friend standing beside me, did not. So there is some validation to that theory, I actually experienced it.

Many spiritualists believe there is a very thin veil between the spirit world and our world. As it gets closer to Halloween this veil gets thinner and thinner. So by October 31st they say the dead can cross over into our dimension. This is why I believe I was able to photograph so much activity when I was in Salem on October 30 and October31st, Halloween. Especially, when we were walking around the Howard Street Cemetery.

According to the International Ghost Hunters Society, they believe this cemetery is a doorway into another dimension where good and evil can pass through. There is an entrance and exit, so it is open to any type of spirits during this time.

Irish immigrants brought the custom of Halloween to America in the 1840's. Originally, the Celts believed that the souls of the spirits would come back during Halloween to possess the bodies of the living for the next year. So on October 31st, the Celts would dress up in costumes to ward off these evil spirits. Halloween did not originate from evil practices. It started in the Catholic Church. This was a day to honor the saints. It was called "All Hallows Day', or "All Saints Day". November 1st was called "All Hallows Eve". In Celtic Ireland, October 31st was the day their summer ended. This was considered the Celtic New Year. Overtime, this holiday adopted the name "Halloween", and it became more ceremonial. The belief of possession dissipated and the act of dressing up became more traditional.

Whether, you've had a ghostly encounter or not, I hope this book provides you with an insight into the realm of the unknown. Perhaps you may think twice the next time you are alone and you feel like someone is watching you or standing behind you. Could it be a presence of a ghost? Or just the product of imagination? You decide. Perhaps it's just a lonely spirit trying to make contact with those who are sensitive to their energy.

SECTION I

Ghostly Dream Visitations

MY MOTHER
1/13/79

My mother passed away of cancer when I was 9 years old. She suffered for 3 months, and then died suddenly one winter day in her sleep. I loved her so much and we were very close. I was devastated and thought I couldn't live without her. This probably was the beginning of my fascination with death and the paranormal. I wanted to know if there was life after death. I wanted to know if somehow she could contact me and let me know that she was all right. I also wanted to believe in the afterlife and know there is something to look forward to after we die. I couldn't wait to reunite with my mother.

I started reading and researching everything I could on the paranormal. I still read today, almost everyday for at least an hour a day on this subject.

On January 13, 1979, my father went to go visit my mother at Sloan Kettering Hospital in NYC. When he was about to leave to let her rest, he glanced over at her, and she smiled back at him, then she waved her hand and said goodbye. My father smiled and waved back. He said to me that he thought it was a little strange because she would always say to him, "I'll see you tomorrow", she never would say goodbye. He remembered that fateful night like it was yesterday. He said she seemed very peaceful and looked radiant. I think that she was preparing him for the inevitable. She knew she was nearing her end and soon she would die. She wanted him to be happy when he left that night and to remember her as she was before she got sick, a young, beautiful woman full of life.

My father's commute from the hospital in Manhattan to Spring Valley New York, including traffic, would be an average of 3 hours. By the time he got home that night, the phone was ringing non-stop. The doctor was calling to let my father know that my mother had died a few minutes after he had left her room that night.

A few days later after my mother passed away, she came to visit me in my dreams. I had two dreams with her trying to send me a message. In the first dream, I was looking up in the sky and I saw my mother driving a convertible. She pulled in front of me and was smiling and looked very happy. She looked normal, like the way she did before she got sick. She asked me if I wanted to go for a ride. I was so happy to see her; I couldn't believe my eyes. I said "mommy how can this be? I thought you died? Are you a ghost? "She said "I'm not dead I will always be with you in spirit". Then we drove around the sky for awhile looking at all the beautiful white puffy clouds. She looked at me and said she was running out of time, and had to go. When she dropped me off she said "don't cry, I will see you again." After that, I felt a little better.

The second dream I had with her was about a year later. I dreamt that I was inside a grocery store in the frozen food section looking for ice cream. All of a sudden, I saw my mother walking towards me. She was wearing a gray sweat suit. She unzipped her jacket and showed me her enormous white angel wings. She was happy and looked very healthy. She wanted to let me know she is an angel now and not to grieve or worry about her anymore. I felt an overwhelming sense of happiness after talking to her. I went to hug her, and then she told me she didn't have a lot of time and she had to go. Then I woke up.

I remember years before my mother got sick, she would always sing me to sleep. She would say "Please remember, if I die before you, don't worry, I will be waiting for you at the gates of heaven and some day you will come join me and we will be together again". I would tell her not to say that because she was never going to die. Then she would sing me to sleep. Looking back now, it seemed like she knew her time would soon end.

MY GRANDFATHER
1985

In 1986, I was about 16 years old, when my grandfather passed away. I also had a dream that he visited me. This was a few days after his funeral. It was a Sunday tradition for the whole family to get together and have dinner.

In the dream, everyone was sitting around the table eating and talking with the exception of my grandfather. He was standing up behind everyone. He had his arms extended patting the shoulders of my grandmother and aunt. He was looking at me smiling. He acted like everything was ok, just like any other Sunday. I couldn't believe he was there; it seemed so real, not like he just passed away a few days prior. I felt like he was letting me know that he was all right. I think this was his way of saying goodbye.

GUADALUPE
2000

In August 2000, I was living with my boyfriend Moises, at the time, in Dingmans Ferry, Pennsylvania.

One night I had fallen asleep about midnight when suddenly something woke me from a deep sleep around 3:00am. I sat up abruptly, and felt an overwhelming sense of sadness. I was overcome with emotion and started crying hysterically. I was so sad and I didn't know why. I felt like something horrible had happened but I didn't know what it could be. I then felt a cold breeze blow throughout the room. I checked to see if a window was open, but they where all shut tight. My boyfriend reassured me that everything was ok, and he said "just go back to sleep, you where probably dreaming. " I listened to him and eventually I drifted off.

The next day my boyfriend left work early to come see me. He was crying and he got down on his knees to hug me. I was worried because I have never seen him like this before. I asked him what was wrong. Then he told me he got a phone call telling him his mother Guadalupe, had passed away the night before. She was living in Venezuela, Guatemala in a nursing home. She had been sick for a long time and was dying of stomach cancer. He asked the nurse what time she had passed away and she replied 3:00am. This was the same time that I woke up the night before.

I think his mother was trying to contact me, so she could relay a message to her son. She wanted to say goodbye. I didn't know her very well, because she lived in a foreign country and didn't speak any English. I only met her once and we couldn't understand each other. She just smiled and nodded her head. I know she had a strong bond with her son and she loved him very much. I sensed she was a beautiful, caring person. Although this was a sad tragic event, I am glad that she contacted me so that I could comfort her son in his time of grief.

SECTION II

Personal Experiences

THE OLD LADY IN THE ROCKING CHAIR

SPRING VALLEY - NEW YORK
1977

The first time I experienced ghostly phenomenon was in 1977. I was seven years old. I encountered poltergeist activity ay my cousin's house and I saw an apparition of an old women in my bedroom. I was living in an apartment complex in Spring Valley, New York. I was lying in bed trying to fall asleep. I glanced over and saw a figure of an old woman hunched over sitting at the edge of my bed. She looked very real. She had white hair pulled back and her clothing was dark. It looked like she was wearing a shawl and a dress. She never spoke; she just looked ahead with a vacant stare. It looked like she was sitting in a rocking chair, moving back and forth. This was odd because there was only a regular chair at the foot of the bed.

I looked away in fright, and put my head under the blankets. I then peeked out hoping she was gone, but she was still there. I yelled over to my brother, who was sharing the room at the time, to see if he saw the old woman also. He said "yes". We both couldn't believe it. She seemed to appear for a long time. We both put our heads in and out of the covers until she finally disappeared. I started screaming, so my father came to see what was wrong. Of course, by the time he arrived the apparition was gone.

Once again she reappeared briefly after my father had left the room.

This time I wasn't scared. She seemed to be kind and sad. I didn't sense anything evil. It was almost as if she were watching over us like a guardian. She looked over at us and smiled. Then suddenly she disappeared and we never saw her again.

I think she only wanted to appear to my brother and myself since we were children. Usually children and animals are more susceptible to the paranormal then adults. Since children don't know too much about ghosts they have an unbiased point of view. They are more open to everything and are more likely to see a ghost then an adult. They react to what they see or feel. If she appeared in front of my father, he would probably dismiss this as his imagination. Therefore, we were likely to believe more in the existence of this old woman then my parents.

She never appeared again to either one of us. We moved away shortly after the incident.

THE DEVIL

SPRING VALLEY - NEW YORK
1977

After I saw the apparition of the old lady in my bedroom, I saw another frightening figure in my room. I think it occurred about a week later.

I was falling asleep, and I glanced over to my right side. I saw some white mist rising up from the floor. It began to take shape and materialized into a monster. It looked like the devil. The figure was red; it had a black mustache and beard, pointy ears and eyes. On its head were horns and long talons on its fingertips. Its upper body and chest was very muscular and looked like a regular man, however it was just a head and torso floating above my bed. It didn't have a lower body or legs. Then it started growling and laughing and coming closer to me.

I started screaming and yelling for my parents. When they rushed in the room, the devil figure vanished instantly.

I remember seeing it again, a few days later. It appeared to rise from the same spot in the floor. It rose above my bed and started talking to me. I ran out of the room and into the kitchen, where my parents were standing. I was hysterical shouting "I saw the devil", "I saw the devil". "It was in my room, next to my bed."

I insisted that they check it out. They rushed into the bedroom, but by then the devil figure was gone. They never believed me, but I know what I saw was real. I think that apartment was haunted. The evil entity that was there preyed on my darkest fears, which in my case, was the devil. Since I was a child, in my mind, this is what the stereo-typical devil looked like. It probably would have appeared as something different to my brother or parents. It would have taken on the form of what they were most frightened of.

I'm not sure if it was really the devil that I saw, or one of his demons. All I know is that it had a profound effect on me and I didn't remember the incident until many years later. We didn't live in that apartment very long. My mother passed away, and we moved out shortly after. I never found out the truth to what I saw.

THE DAYLIGHT GHOST

SPARROWBUSH - NEW YORK
1987

I didn't see a ghost for a long time. Many years passed, and I forgot about what I had seen previously, until one sunny day.

I was now living in Sparrowbush, New York in 1987. I was seventeen years old and in High School. I had a part-time job after school working at adeli. My job was about two miles from my house. Since I didn't have transportation, I had to walk to work. I would take a short -cut that branched off the main road and went through a cemetery.

Since it was daytime, I wasn't afraid to walk this way. I had traveled this route numerous times. It wasn't until nighttime that I felt a little uneasy.

One day, when I was on my way to work, I approached a figure about 100 yards away. As I walked closer, I saw that it was a woman with long blonde hair and a flowing white gown. She was dressed in Victorian clothing. I could only see her profile. She seemed to be young, in her 20's or early 30's. She seemed to be gliding very fast towards a tombstone. She was only looking forward and oblivious to her surroundings. This could have been a residual haunting. This is when a ghost keeps repeating the same actions that occurred at the time of their death. I glanced over to my left, to see if she had a car, but there wasn't one. She probably walked here from the opposite direction I was coming from. I thought she was just visiting a grave, so I didn't think anything of it. When I looked back at her, she was gone. She just vanished into thin air. I couldn't believe it. I only diverted my eyes for a second.

This was amazing, scary, and shocking. I ran to the tombstone that she was walking towards. I thought maybe she cut through the woods to get to the main road. Then I looked behind the gravestone. There was a very steep cliff followed by a wooded area. There was no way she could have climbed down the hill that fast. She would have torn her clothing and possibly suffered injuries.

That's when I realized she was a ghost. I couldn't believe I saw an apparition in broad daylight. Could this be a lonely wandering spirit visiting a grave of a loved one? Or did she die tragically there on the road? I never found out.

Of course when I arrived at work, I told my friends what I had seen. They just laughed. I didn't think they would believe me. Once again, I doubted myself. This incident triggered my memory. This is when I remembered about 10years earlier when I had seen the ghosts at my cousins and my old apartment.

ANGELIC EYES

MIDDLETOWN - NEW YORK
1987

There was a period of my life when I was very depressed. This was in 1987 when I was in 17 years old. I was sad because I didn't have a good job, a car, or a serious relationship. I was still living home with my parents. I felt very lonely and wondered when my life would improve.

One day my friend and I decided to drive to Middletown, New York to go shopping. It was about a 45-minute drive to all the shopping plazas. She picked me up and we were off.

When we arrived we stopped at an intersection. I was in the passenger seat looking out the window. I glanced over and saw an old woman with long white hair. She looked about 70 years old. I could only see the back of her. She was pulling a cart filled with groceries across the street. She was walking across a dirt walkway that was filled with rocks and she seemed to be struggling. The street she crossed was a very busy intersection. There weren't any houses visible in that area, only shopping plazas and stores.

I remember feeling sorry for her. I though to myself, this poor old woman doesn't have a car or anyone to help her with those groceries. At that moment, she looked up, turned her head, and stared directly at me. She had the brightest clear blue eyes that I have ever seen. Then she smiled, as if she was telling me not to worry, everything would be all right. I took this as a sign of better things to come.

All of a sudden my spirits were lifted, I got an overwhelming feeling of happiness and believed my life would soon get better.

I thought to myself, if this old lady can get by and still remain happy, so can I.

The light turned green, and we proceeded on our way. I turned around to glance once more at the old woman but she was nowhere to be seen. She just seemed to vanish into thin air. I couldn't believe my eyes. Where could she have gone so quickly? There weren't any houses or walkways in that area. There was only the highway in four directions. There was no place that she could have gone in the matter of seconds that I glanced back. I was astonished.

I asked my friend, "Did you see that old lady?" She replied, "What old lady?" That answered my question. I can't believe she didn't notice her. Was she really there?

Had I just seen a ghost? Or was this my guardian angel? She had angelic qualities. Her face was so beautiful and her skin was so smooth like white porcelain. It made her look so young. She seemed very happy and peaceful.

Whether or not she was a ghost or an angel, she definitely left a profound effect on me. I thought about the incident years later. This also peaked my interest in the paranormal. Eventually, my life did get better. She made me think differently and have a more positive outlook on life. I just needed a little encouragement from beyond.

VIRGINIA'S HOUSE

SPARROWBUSH - NEW YORK
1987

A weird incident happened to me when I was 17 years old. I was on a date with my high school boyfriend and I was sitting in the passenger seat of his car. He was taking me home after a movie. He pulled up in front of my house to drop me off. He leaned over to give me a kiss goodnight and his face brushed across my ear, knocking one of my earrings off. We both heard a ping as it fell between the seats. Since it was late and neither of us had a flashlight, he said he would look for the earring in the morning. I agreed and went inside.

The next day, I called him and he said that he couldn't find the earring anywhere. I had taken the other one off the night before, and left it on my dresser in the bedroom. That one also mysteriously disappeared. I looked everywhere but I couldn't find the earrings.

About a week later my best friend, Virginia called me; I had told her about the missing earrings because I was so upset. She asked me what the earrings looked like. I described them to her. They were small, gold, heart-shaped earrings. Then she said, "well when I came home today after school, I saw two shiny gold pieces in the center of my room". "When I picked them up I noticed they were gold heart shaped earrings". My heart started pounding with excitement. I had been so upset and I thought I would never find them. They were very sentimental to me because my boyfriend gave them to me on my birthday.

Then I thought to myself, how this could be, I remember one earring fell between the seats and the other was lost at my house.

I told her I would come right over to see if they were the same earrings. When I got to her house, she showed them to me, I was amazed. They were definitely the same pair that I had lost a week before. At first, I thought it was a joke that they were both playing on me. My friend kept insisting that it wasn't and even she felt spooked out.

I called my boyfriend to tell him that the earrings were found. When I told him they were in the middle of Virginia's bedroom floor, he couldn't believe it. He then asked me if I was playing a trick on him. I also denied it. He is a very skeptical person and does not believe in the paranormal. He found it hard to comprehend that this could possibly happen. He could not find any rational explanation for how the earrings were lost in his car and then appeared in a bedroom. At first he thought I was joking with him about the whole story. I was not. We never found out how this could have possibly happened or why it did. I was just glad that the earrings were found.

Another strange incident that occurred at Virginia's house was that she heard knocking at her bedroom door several nights in a row. This happened on a regular basis. There would always be three knocks and when she opened up the door no one was there. Some theories suggest that knocking sounds are a warning sign from a spirit. Three knocks at a door implies that something negative is about to happen such as death. A few years later her mother passed away in her house.

I think that perhaps my friend had a ghost in her house. I was there so often, it could have followed me home. It could have taken my earrings and brought them back to her house. Some playful ghosts tend to do this, usually a child ghosts looking for attention. Another theory could be that there was a portal into another dimension located in her room. This is an entryway from one world or higher plane into another. This passageway allows a spirit or several to enter into our world.

Another eerie thing that occurred at Virginia's house was when she purchased a gargoyle doorknocker at an old five & dime store on Jersey Avenue in Port Jervis, New York. The five and dime store used to be a JC Newberry, Woolworth's, and a JC Penney catalog center many years ago. Since the doorknocker was on consignment there was really no way to find out who owned it previously. Shortly after purchasing it, she hung it at the foot of her bed and started experiencing knocking sounds at night.

We used to joke around and say that the doorknocker was causing the unexplainable knocks coming from her door. Sometimes in the middle of the night, she would hear three knocks at her door, and then the door would fly open. I also heard it a few times when I was sleeping over. We always assumed it was her sister trying to play a trick on us. Then we would just go back to bed. Until one night, we heard the knocks but her sister wasn't home. That's when we started thinking that the doorknocker was causing these strange occurrences.

This happened back in the 80's, and Virginia has moved a few times since then. She had packed this doorknocker away many years ago. Recently, she moved back to Port Jervis, New York and has hung it up on a wall in her new house. After doing this, she started experiencing strange occurrences in her new home. The house is over 100 years old and used to be a physician's office. She has heard noises in the upstairs bedroom many times.

One night something startling woke her up. She heard the sound of footsteps walking up the stairs, someone enter her bedroom, and then she felt a presence sit down at the edge of her bed. The incident scared her so much, that she decided to move downstairs.

In 2007, I saw the same doorknocker in a catalog. I immediately thought of Virginia. I laughed to myself. We lost contact and I hadn't spoken to her in about 8 years. I started having dreams about her more and more until about a month ago. Finally, a mutual friend said she was trying to get in touch with me. I couldn't believe it. We always seemed to have a psychic connection. We started emailing each other and I finally got a chance to speak to her. My dreams were a foreshadowing of us to make contact again. It was like a premonition. She told me about the experience with the doorknocker. I had told her that was a strange coincidence because I just saw the same doorknocker in a catalog.

Could this doorknocker be a haunted object? Or could it be a ghost following her from a previous house? Sometimes the energy of a spirit can go into an object and possess it. When this object is brought into a house some paranormal activity may occur. The second theory I have is that a ghost can attach itself to a person and follow them around. Especially, if the person is sensitive to the paranormal. They act like a conductor by opening themselves up and allowing ghosts to latch on. The spirit may be drawn to a certain person because they feel that they will see or hear them. Maybe, Virginia has a sixth sense that the spirits pick up on. This could be why she has experienced reoccurring paranormal activity in both houses.

FRED'S HOUSE

PORT JERVIS - NEW YORK
1990

I had a good friend in High School named Fred. When I would go home to visit from college, sometimes I would stay at his house. I remember one scary incident that happened in his house. I had just come home from a long 3-½-hr trip and I was exhausted. Normally, when I stayed over his house, I would sleep in the living room on the couch. Since it was daylight, and there were a few people in the house, he suggested that I sleep in his bedroom. I agreed that was a good idea. Within a few minutes I drifted off to sleep.

As I was starting to dream, I could hear slight whispering near my head. The sound seemed to be coming from behind me, in the corner of the room. Then it sounded like men and women talking very loudly in a conversation. I couldn't make out what they were saying. They were mumbling at first, then the voices seemed to be getting louder and louder. The voices eventually escalated in to shouting my name in my ear. It sounded like a bunch of people were standing over me trying to wake me up. I thought my friends were playing a trick on me. I woke up and looked around the room. I didn't see anything unusual. I tried to fall back to sleep. I dismissed the incident as a dream.

I finally fell back to sleep and the shouting started again. It was so loud that I woke up again. Then the room was an eerie silence. The voices stopped instantaneously when I was awake.

At this point, I was truly terrified and ran out of Fred's bedroom into the living room. My two friends were sitting on the couch watching television. Fred looked at the expression on my face and said; "did you hear the voices too?" I said; "yes, I think your house is haunted." He admitted to me that he as well as a mutual friend had also slept in that room and heard the awful voices. He didn't warn me of this because he wanted to see if I would have the same experience. Fred also said that he has slept in other rooms in the house but has never experienced anything abnormal. The only ghostly phenomenon that has occurred was in his bedroom. No other incidents have occurred since that day. We never did find out if the house was haunted.

Eventually, Fred moved out of that house and returned to his hometown, Chapel Hill, North Carolina. I returned to Suny Morrisville College, and forgot about the incident until many years later.

THE OUIJA BOARD

SUNY MORRISVILLE - NEW YORK
1990

I went to college at Suny Morrisville, New York from September 1989 to May 1991. I had a bunch of friends that were interested in the supernatural. We would get together occasionally and hold séances in our dorm room. We would use the Ouija Board. This device is used to contact the spirits of the dead.

The Ouija Board has black letters and a planchette. It has the alphabet and the words YES, NO, and GOODBYE on it. When you begin, you place your fingers on the planchette and then you can ask the board questions. Two or three people can hold a séance. Three people are preferred because one can write down the words and decipher them while the other two keep the board going. If they take their hands off, they may break the connection of energy between the players and the spirits.

You must be very careful when using the Ouija Board. It is rumored to be a doorway into another dimension. If you use the board, it may open a portal which good spirits as well as evil spirits may enter into our world.

Sometimes if you go looking for evil, you might possibly find it. When using the board, be careful not to invite unwanted spirits into this world. A malevolent spirit can attach itself to you, causing trouble for the rest of your life. It is very hard to send this kind of spirit back to where it came from. The doorway to the other dimension is difficult to close. Evil spirits can lie and deceive. They can trick you into seeing what you want to believe. You cannot believe everything that the board spells out. Try to find evidence about what you're being told is the truth.

The evil spirits don't always come through to communicate. Sometimes they may cause fear or inflict negative spirit activity. This can't happen just by simply talking to them through the board. However, there is a higher chance that his could happen if you invite the spirits into this world. It's recommended to say prayers to protect you before using the board. Also you must be open minded and willing to accept whatever comes through. You should treat the spirits with respect and ask if anyone would like to come forth and talk. Don't expect for the board and the spirits to work every time. It takes alot of energy on both sides to keep the séance going. So if a spirit is having a hard time communicating or points to the word "GOODBYE", then you should let it go. Then the next step would be for you to place the planchette also on the word "GOODBYE", and tell it you are now leaving. This closes the board.

When my friends and I were asking questions while using the board, we contacted a spirit of a little boy. He said his name was Leroy. He was eight years old, and lived in the 1800's. He said he died during an operation but he wasn't sure what kind. This was a little eerie and sad. He seemed sweet and we felt great sorrow for him since he departed from this world at such a young age. We couldn't believe he was trapped in our dimension for so long.

Suddenly we lost contact and it was hard to find him again. Another spirit came through and took his place. This spirit wasn't friendly and gave us very limited information on its identity. It kept spelling out the name "MaryAnn". We continued to ask questions, but it never answered any of them. It then gave us a message to "Open the door, MaryAnn". Then we all heard three knocks at our bedroom door. We looked at each other but no one was willing to open it. We were all too frightened of the outcome. I glanced at my roommate who looked very scared and nervous. We decided not to play with the Ouija Board anymore.

My roommate started crying and told us that before she was born her mother was pregnant. She had a miscarriage and lost her baby. She was going to name it "MaryAnn". This could have been a coincidence, but we were too startled and too sad to pick up the board again.

I didn't play with the Ouija Board again until I was twenty eight years old. This time my friend Joann asked the board about marriage and children. I didn't want to know my future so I didn't ask it anything. It told her she would marry a man named Joe, and have one son who had blonde hair and blue eyes. About a year later, she did end up married to someone named Joe and had a son with the same characteristics that the board told her. This emphasized my belief that the board is connected to the other side. Luckily everything worked out for her.

I still wasn't sure if the Ouija Board was good or evil or maybe a little of both. So why take a chance with interfering with the future. I haven't picked up the board since.

CHANNELING

SUNY MORRISVILLE - NEW YORK
1990

Another incident that happened to me occurred when I was in college. I was trying to develop my sixth sense. I was working in an office under the college work study program. I answered phones, typed memos, filed and made copies of reports and tests. I discovered one day that if I closed my eyes and concentrated, I could file quicker and easier.

I was given a list of names with a stack of paperwork that had to be filed. I would look at the list and once I found the names, I would put the paperwork in their corresponding files. This was very time consuming, so I wanted to devise an easier way to do this.

One day when I was filing, I noticed I felt tingling vibrations in my left hand when I ran my fingers along the tops of the files. I also felt a little sensation of heat at my fingertips. The next day I decided to do a little experiment. I closed my eyes and concentrated on the name of the person's file I was looking for. While I was repeating the name to myself, I ran my left hand over the files. The tingling vibrations would get stronger and the heat more intense in certain spots. I would stop my hand at the place where I felt the most energy. Then I would look down and pull up the file. This file would be the name I was looking for. I was amazed. I tried to do this again. At first, I only found the files a few times. Then the more I practiced, the better I got. Eventually, I could find the files every time I did this.

I believe this was a way of channeling my abilities or developing my sixth sense. This energy that I felt has gotten stronger over the years. This is the same energy that I feel when I am in a haunted place. I pick up the energy of the ghosts that are present. This is why I started taking photographs of haunted places. I wanted to get some scientific proof that what I was feeling was definitely the presence of a ghost.

The sixth sense is a heightened awareness that is beyond our normal five senses. The five senses are sight, hearing, smell, taste, and touch. Everyone has the sixth sense but some are more sensitive to it then others. This sense is considered an extra-sensory perception. It is often at times very unpredictable. Most people have experienced the sixth sense without realizing it, some examples of the sixth sense are:

1) Some dreams you may have, actually come true. Experiencing déjà vu or the felling that you been through this before.
2) Anytime you had a hunch or feeling that something was going to happen and it did.
3) Times when you have thought of the same thing at the same time as another person.
4) Anytime you felt a presence of someone or something when they are not there.

People who have experienced some of these things are considered to have the sixth sense. These people are also very sensitive to the paranormal. There is a higher chance that they will experience something paranormal in their lifetime. I am one of those people. This is why I believe I have been able to capture so much paranormal activity on film. I think this is how I am channeling my abilities now that I am older.

CORNFIELD

SOUTH CENTERVILLE - NEW YORK
1994

One night my friend and I were driving home from a concert. It was very late probably around 3:00AM. We decided to take a shortcut home. The back road we took was through South Centerville, New York. We were traveling on Route 6, heading towards Port Jervis. On this road, there is a high school and across from it, there is a cornfield.

It was very cold and dark that night. It was mid October and the moon or stars weren't visible. As the car approached the cornfield, I glanced over to the right side and looked out the window. I saw an old man. He was leaning forward into the road, almost falling over. He looked very pale, gaunt, and like a skeleton. He had a very pronounced Adam's apple and hollow cheekbones. His clothes were baggy and looked like they could slip right off him. He was just standing hunched over staring straight ahead. When our car passed him we both looked over to see where he was going. It was a little creepy.

This man seemed to come out of nowhere. There were no houses or cars around. It's like he came out of the cornfield. What would an old man be doing standing on the edge of the road in the middle of the night? We'll we didn't stay around long enough to find out. When we drove past him, I noticed my friend looked over at him and then sped up to get away faster. I turned around to take a second glance and he seemed to vanish into thin air. The sighting happened within seconds. It scared us both and we didn't travel that road for many years.

BLESSED BE

SALEM - MASSACHUSETTS
1998–2006

For many years something always summoned me to go to Salem, Massachusetts. The first few years that I traveled there, I didn't know the roads very well, so I would always end up getting lost. Strangely, I would end up in a two mile radius of the Old Jail, Howard Street Cemetery and the site of the original Witch Dungeon. It was kind of eerie.

One time, I parked my car on Essex Street in front of a parking meter, which was in this vicinity. There was about an hour left on the meter, so I put a few quarters in for two more hours, so it registered 3 hours. My friend Janet and I were gone four hours but when we came back to the car it only registered that we were gone for 1 hour. It was bizarre. It seemed like something was preventing us from leaving. Since we had the extra time, we decided to stay longer.

We had been parked in front of an old book store. We now had time to check it out. As soon as I walked in the store, I was automatically drawn to the back of the store. It was as if something was guiding me to walk to a particular spot near the book shelf. I picked up a black book with gold trim around the edges. This book was through a doorway covered by a curtain. It led to a separate room. I was looking at the books and all of a sudden, I felt like a strong presence was there looking at me, I felt extremely nauseous and like I couldn't breathe. The room suddenly became cold, and then I had a horrible feeling of dread come over me. I didn't understand why I felt this way. All I knew was that the feeling was so overwhelming that I had to get out of there. I ran out of the store. Immediately, as soon as I was outside, I felt better. The scary feeling went away and I felt normal again.

Another weird thing that happened to me in Salem was when I bought a Blessed Be bumper sticker from a witchcraft shop. I believe it was in 2001. I put it on my rear bumper and I had a string of bad luck. The first time my car was hit from behind and the sticker was destroyed. Then I went back to the store the following year and purchased another sticker. I put it in my pocket because I was going through a haunted house during Halloween. When I got to the other side, I checked my pocket and the sticker was missing. I didn't see, feel or hear it drop.

In 2002, I went back to the same store and purchased the sticker for the third time and put it on the rear bumper of a different car. My new car was hit again from the rear and estimated that the car was totaled. The sticker was once again shattered into a million pieces. Finally, I began to suspect the sticker was bringing me bad luck. I'm not sure if there was negative energy surrounding the sticker, the store that it was purchased at, or if someone put a spell on it. All I knew was that this was too much of a coincidence. How could this happen that many times? I decided never to purchase that sticker ever again.

The next year my friend Debbie went to Salem with her daughter for "Haunted Happenings". This is a month long festival. There are a lot of vendors and activities on the weekends. When they returned home, her daughter gave me a "Blessed Be" bumper sticker. My mouth dropped open. I said "thank you" and took it, but I didn't tell her my past experiences with it. I kept it for awhile but I never placed it on my car again.

Eventually, I got rid of the sticker with a lot of hesitation. Something made me want to keep it.

In October, the following year, I went with another friend of mine to "Haunted Happenings" in Salem, Massachusetts. Of course, we had another strange experience. We were walking around for a few hours enjoying the festivities. We did a lot of shopping, watched re-enactments of the witch trials, and visited the various witch museums. I was getting tired so we decided to stop at our car and take a little break. I closed my eyes and was dozing off to sleep. Suddenly, I felt the car rock back and forth. It felt like someone was jumping on the back of the bumper rocking the car back and forth.

At first, I though it was some kids playing tricks on us. After all it was Halloween and there were all kinds of drunk, rowdy people around. However, when I looked around there was absolutely no- one there.

I tried to fall asleep again and the same thing happened. My friend said she could feel the car moving also. This scared us, so we finally got out of the car and started walking around Salem again. I was under the impression that something didn't want us there. Perhaps, something bad would have happened if we stayed in the car.

The last major incident that happened to me was when I was in Salem, Massachusetts on October 28, 2005.

I went with my friend, Val, to a ghost photography seminar. The woman giving the presentation was telling us that her house was haunted. She said she discovered her house was inhabited by a little boy who likes to play tricks on her. He would steal things from her, and they would be gone for a few days and the suddenly reappear in the oddest places. One of his favorite things to steal was her car keys. She said that sometimes he follows her wherever she goes.

After we left the seminar, we went to get lunch and I handed my car keys to my friend. It was her turn to drive.

That day in Salem was a little strange because it was snowing heavy and there wasn't any bad weather in the forecast for that day.

Salem is unusual because I have come there in October and sometimes it would be snowing or it could be 85 degrees and humid. Something strange always happens when I'm there.

After lunch, we went to several shops and activities for the rest of the day. It was a Saturday night, and we were getting tired. We decided to head back to our hotel, which was about 40 minutes away in Tewksbury, Massachusetts. My dog, Kiki was patiently waiting for us. My friend started getting nervous and I asked her what was the matter. She said she couldn't find the car keys. I thought she was joking.

We decided to find a phone, and call a cab so we could get back to the hotel. The problem was that I wasn't sure if I had a spare key in the glove compartment. If not, then we would be stranded there until Monday. I lived 5 hours away and I would have to go to a local Toyota dealer and get an extra key made. Since it was Saturday night, the dealership was already closed and it wasn't open on Sunday. We both had to be back on Monday morning to go to work, which was Halloween day. We found a phone at a bagel shop. The owner let us use her personal phone. We told her about our situation and she tried calling her locksmith to see if he could help us. He never called her back. The fire alarm went off in the building while we were waiting. Trucks came and we weren't sure what to do. Luckily, it was a false alarm. There was a psychic convention going on in the plaza and they were burning too much incense which caused the alarm to go off. Looking back now it was kind of funny.

The owner of the bagel shop told us her husband was a former locksmith. She called him to see if he would come help us. He agreed. Since the car was parked on a public road we had to report it to the police. We told them the situation and they said we could leave the car there overnight if we chose to.

The woman's husband picked us up and drove us to my car. He said he could help me get into my car so I could check my glove compartment for a spare key. When he tried to use the Slim Jim on the driver's side window, the glass shattered into a million pieces. The Slim Jim fell right through and landed on the seat. I was so upset because my car was only five months old.

The man was also very upset, so he called a friend to help tow us to our hotel. Since the window was now completely broken, we didn't want to leave the open car on the street. It was Halloween weekend, and there were tons of people around. We were afraid the car would get vandalized.

The man's friend had a hard time moving the car onto the flatbed. He finally got it on and towed my car to the hotel which was about 40 minutes away. I was anxious to get back to the hotel because my dog was in his cage all day. I felt it was safer to have the car with us even though I couldn't drive it. Plus, if we didn't have it towed, we would have to get a cab, and go back into Salem the next day. It would have cost a lot of money for a cab both ways.

We called the police to see if anyone handed in car keys but they said no. We ended up staying another night in the hotel since we couldn't leave anyway. We were stranded there all day on Sunday. To pass the time, we took a walk to Wal-Mart and ate at a restaurant which was nearby. We tried to make the best of it. Monday morning we both had to call our jobs to let them know we were not able to come in. I had to find a Toyota dealer to get a spare key made. Then I had to call my insurance company and see if there was a place in Massachusetts that could fix my window. The dealership said they needed a code to make a spare key. I had this code but it was on my spare car keys in Pennsylvania. I had to call my landlord and see if she could go to my apartment, look for the key, and give me the number over the phone. After we got the code we then had to call a cab to get to the Toyota dealer, get the key made and then go back to the hotel. The cab was coming from a different town, so it was expensive. We discovered that we could have walked to the dealership. It was only about a mile down the road from where we were staying. Of course we didn't know how close it was until after we got there. Meanwhile, we had to check out of the hotel by 11:00am and it was getting close to that time. I had to leave my dog in the car while we went to the dealership. I was worried because of the busted window. I was afraid he might jump out the window or someone might steal him. My dog Kiki is a pug. I've heard horror stories about this sort of thing. I was probably being paranoid but considering all the bad luck we were having, I was just being precautious.

I was on the phone with the insurance company for a few hours when we returned to the hotel. Finally, I was able to find a place that could fix my window that day. I stressed the urgency that it needed to be fixed immediately because I had to get home and I lived five hours away. I told them I had to travel on the highway and it would be extremely difficult without a window. There were also fragments of glass everywhere inside the car. After all the hassle, I was able to get the window fixed and I finally left Salem on Halloween day.

It felt like something was keeping us there and didn't want us to leave. We never found the car keys.

I have a good friend Steve that lives in Medford, Massachusetts. I went to visit him in August of 2006 to say goodbye because I was moving to New Mexico. He lives about a half hour from Salem. I had to convince my friend Val, to go with me to Salem again. Considering what happened to us the previous year she was reluctant to go. She thought we might have bad luck again like we always do.

Steve wanted us to meet his co-worker Stephanie. She does psychic readings and lives in Salem. We got acquainted the day before at his neighborhood block party. We told her we would meet for lunch the next day. We followed Steve to her apartment. I was shocked to see the location of the apartment. As we approached the road closer to the building, I got chills. I looked over at my friend, and we both realized Stephanie lived on the road that we got stranded on the year before. This was on Hubbard Street . We were both afraid to get out of the car. Eventually, we did and for once nothing bad happened.

Stepahnie said that at one time Nathaniel Hawthorne lived in her apartment building. It was only for a short time. He did some writing in the attic. Her apartment is one of the many stops on the local History tour of Salem. We had a nice day. This was the first time I left Salem without anything bad or spooky happening. Could it be because I was there in August and not October? Or could it be that the spell was finally broken? Salem knew this was the last time I would be there. I was leaving Salem and the east coast for good. I was moving to Albuquerque, New Mexico in search for a new adventure into the unknown. I left closing one portal and entered into a new one.

HAUNTED HOUSE IN DINGMANS FERRY

WILD ACRES

DINGMANS FERRY - PENNSLYVANIA
2000

In 2000, I was living in Dingmans Ferry, Pennsylvania with my boyfriend at the time. We lived in a development called Wild Acres. It was located in a private gated community.

The house was a small A- frame with two small bedrooms, 1 small bathroom and kitchen, a medium sized living room, and a full basement. The house was inexpensive and we were excited to move in.

One of the first strange incidents that occurred was while I was painting my bedroom. My first project was to lay primer down on the walls to get it ready for the teal color paint that I selected. The room was empty and only had paint, rollers, and brushes in it. The only thing that I placed in my bedroom window was an incense burner. I walked into the other room for just a minute and when I returned I noticed the incense burner had been moved. This was weird because I was the only one in the house. I dismissed it thinking maybe I just moved it without realizing and forgot about it. Then the next day, I felt like someone was staring at me. I glanced over my shoulder but I didn't see anything. Then later on that evening, I discovered that the incense burner was missing. I could not find it anywhere. It mysteriously reappeared several days later back where I had originally placed it. I was a little surprised, but more intrigued then scared.

My boyfriend worked two jobs and he would get home very late and I would already be sleeping when he arrived. I didn't like to be in the house alone so I would invite my friend to stay over on the weekends.

The house had many problems. In the bathroom, mold was growing on the walls. I would scrap the paint and the mold spots off and then repaint the walls. It would grow back only a few days later. I did this twice, and then I finally gave up. It was useless to keep trying to fix this reoccurring problem. The sinks were always clogged and the basement was very damp and smelled like stale air. I was allergic to mold so I was always sick with a sinus infection. This was not a good environment for me to live in.

One night, I heard a fluttering of wings in the wall of my bedroom. It scared me but I was sure there had to be an explanation for it. The next day, I discovered, there was a small hole in the wall from the outside leading to the wall in my bedroom. I saw a hummingbird squeeze through and fly in. I found the culprit. We also found mice in the house. They left droppings in my shoes, and chewed up some of my books in the closet. In the kitchen I found dog food next to my utensils. The mice were taking the dog food and storing it away in the drawers. At first I thought it was funny, but then it became annoying. I could hear them at night rustling around.

I had a separate bedroom because my boyfriend had long work hours and I didn't want him waking me up every night at 2:00am. I had to get up at 6:00am. I also felt a little creepy when I was in his bedroom. I didn't like to sleep in there. Ever since we moved in I felt like there was a presence in the house. It seemed to be concentrated in the living room and my boyfriend's bedroom. That's where I felt the presence the strongest. It didn't feel like anything evil or threatening. It just felt like I was never alone and somebody else was living there with us.

Another strange thing that kept occurring was that when I returned home from work, I would find every single cabinet door in the kitchen wide open. I know that they were all shut when I left in the morning. I asked my boyfriend if he did this. He insisted that it wasn't him. I would yell at him and say you were probably too tired too remember that you left them open. This happened several times. One night I was cooking dinner and one of the cabinet doors opened slowly behind me. It scared me a little but I knew nothing bad would happen. This is when I was convinced that the house was haunted.

I asked my boyfriend about the previous owners. I found out that the woman who lived here before us had a husband who just recently died of a heart attack. That's why she sold the house. He was a physician. This was their weekend getaway house. Sometimes he would come there by himself to go hunting and fishing on the weekend and he would stay there. She didn't tell us whether or not her husband passed away in the house, but I believe that he did.

I have taken pictures of my dog in the living room and several orbs have shown up surrounding him. I think he could also sense a presence there.

I wonder if the doctor enjoyed the house so much and the piece and quiet of the neighborhood that he may have never wanted to leave. I think it was his presence that I felt when I was in the house.

(Kiki with orbs above him and on the right side)
Wild Acres Dingmans Ferry, Pa. 5/2000

HAUNTED HOUSE IN MATAMORAS

MATAMORAS - PENNSYLVANIA
2000

I believe that animals have a sixth sense. They feel when a presence is around. Sometimes the spirits are drawn to them because they remind them of the pets they once had during their lifetime. As I mentioned before there were orbs surrounding my dog Kiki. These strange anomalies appeared again at another house that I lived in. This house was located in Matamoras, Pennsylvania near the Delaware River.

The house's original structure was on the lower floor. The upstairs rooms and hallway were added on many years later. I lived upstairs where there wasn't any paranormal activity. Strange things only seemed to happen downstairs near the bathroom and fireplace. Every time I walked into this room it felt a little eerie. It was a strange uneasy feeling that I sensed while sitting near the fireplace on the couch. When I approached the bathroom I also experienced this same feeling. The bathroom had an old-fashioned porcelain bath tub with claw-like talons on the bottom of the four corners. Next to the bathroom was a stairway that led to the second floor. Since the upstairs was added on, when you opened the door it led into a bedroom closet, which was in my room. I think it opened up into a big room at one time. The closet was built later on, but the stairs were never removed. It was a weird design. We never used this stairway; it was blocked off downstairs by a wooden board.

This house dates back to the early 1800's. It was an old Masonry's shop at one time and a Masonic Temple years later. The house was made into a rental and then put up for sale. I'm not sure who lived there before me or if anything bad happened there. Orbs appeared surrounding my dog in some of the photos that were taken downstairs near the fireplace. I didn't realize this until many years later, when I was moving and looking through all of my photos. Then I realized that these orbs could be an indication of paranormal activity.

Another time, at my friend's house I took a picture of my dog chasing their cat. However, it was outside on the deck. When I took a closer look at the picture I noticed an orb appeared beside my dog. Maybe the spirits like my dog so much they follow him wherever he goes. Or it could be the same spirit from the house in Dingmans attached to him. After all, Kiki stayed in the same bedroom that the doctor did. I think my dog, Kiki has been haunted most of his life. He is such a sociable dog that not only does he have human companions, but ghost companions as well.

(Kiki and my friend Janet, downstairs)
Matamoras, Pa. 9/99
(There is an orb above Kiki)

Kiki and Hopper
(Orb appears above Kiki)
Shohola, Pa. 8/2000

THE EXORCIST STAIRWAY TO HELL

GEORGETOWN - WASHINGTON
2001

Many years ago, in July 2001, I went with my friend, Janet, to Washington, DC on vacation. We decided to go to the old historic district of Georgetown. It was a beautiful stroll walking on the cobblestones and viewing the Victorian buildings, shops, and restaurants. I wanted to visit the sites and see the famous steps where one of the ending scenes from the movie the "Exorcist" was filmed. This is when the demon possesses the priest and jumps out the window. He topples down a long set of concrete steps and cracks his head open dying in the street. I was excited and anxious to photograph these steps in hope of catching some paranormal anomaly on film.

The Exorcist, released in 1973, was a movie about a young girl who gets possessed by an evil demon. The mother turns to a priest for help. He then gets the Catholic Church involved. He, along with another priest performs an exorcism on the young girl. Her face contorts looking demonic; she vomits uncontrollably, levitates, curses, and speaks in tongues. She is very violent towards her mother and the priests. There are some very lewd and shocking scenes in the movie. The voice of the demon is so deep and scary it is hard to believe a young girl is saying such vulgar things.

There was so much controversy surrounding the film. Many strange occurrences happened during the filming of this movie.

As I recall from watching an interview and reading several articles, there were a lot of strange incidents that occurred on the set. There was a fire that caused the filming to be shut down for a few days. Sometimes the temperature was very cold in the studio, a couple of actors died during the filming, a few actors were hurt and the director acted a little crazy. His approach was very unconventional. He literally scared the hell out of the actors in the process of directing the movie. He would shoot a rifle up in the air and do various other techniques in order to shock and scare the actors and then film their reaction. This was genuine fear on their faces during certain scenes. This is what made the movie look so authentic.

I saw this movie when I was 9 years old. My parents advised me against watching it. That made me even more curious to see why it was so scary. The night that I watched the movie, I was terrified. I was very nervous, nauseous, dizzy, and was vomiting. I thought I was becoming possessed. The movie scared me so much that it haunted me for 3 years after I had watched it. I couldn't sleep at night, and when I did I had several scary nightmares. I felt anxious and alone. This was during a rough time in my life. My mother had just passed away, we moved, and my father got remarried. My stress level was so high at the time that I am sure this is why the movie had such a profound effect on me.

Years went by and I was no longer scared by this movie, only fascinated. I found out many years later that the famous steps were located in Georgetown. My curiosity intensified, so I decided to find them and take photographs of the steps. I noticed a wall along the sidewalk with a painting of the steps and a short story behind the filming of the "Exorcist".

I wasn't sure exactly where they were located. Janet and I were walking on the sidewalk and suddenly I got a strange feeling. I felt like something was drawing me to a particular spot. When I stopped walking and looked up, I saw the scary stairway.

As I approached the steps I was a little scared. They were not in the dark, gloomy, area that I expected. The steps are located between an Exxon gas station on the left, and a small park on the right. In the movie, it looked like a dark alleyway with nothing surrounding it but the house towering over the long stairway.

I got startled as I took a picture standing at the bottom of the steps looking up. All of a sudden, as I was about to photograph the steps, a jogger appeared at the top and started running down towards me. I felt uneasy and thought the steps were cursed. I was afraid to touch them. I snapped three photos of the eerie steps. It was a clear, hot, summer night so the pictures should have come out perfect. However, this was not the case.

When I went to pick up the film, I was anxious to see the steps. I was shocked when I realized that all the pictures of the steps weren't there. They were never developed and appeared to be all black. There were no images present. At first I thought it was the film. Sometimes the end of the role gets exposed and doesn't develop properly. In the beginning of the role of film were pictures of the Washington monuments, then the steps, and then there were pictures of scenery at the end of the role. All the photos prior to and after the steps came out very clear and in focus. I thought that it was strange that the only pictures that didn't come out were the eerie steps that were in the middle of the role of film. I was disappointed because I was hoping to show my friends at work evidence of paranormal activity.

It seemed something didn't want me to photograph these steps. Was it just a coincidence or was it the same evil energy associated with the movie causing the film not to be developed? This strange phenomenon adds to the mystery of the bad luck surrounding the making of the movie.

FROM BEYOND THE GRAVE

ELECTRICAL DISTURBANCES
JUNE 2008

During the writing of this book, the son of a close friend of mine passed away suddenly. It was very traumatic. He died in his sleep from an accidental overdose of a combination of prescription drugs. He left behind a wife, whom he was separated from and a two year old daughter.

When his father found out what happened he was grief stricken. It was very sad and shocking to me, even though, I didn't know him very well. He was more of an acquaintance but I did talk to him a few times. It was very sad because he was young and finally started getting his life together.

That day, a few hours later after I heard the horrible news, my cell phone rang. The display on the cell said call from UNKNOWN. I answered it after the second ring, thinking maybe it was my friend Jenna, with some information about the sudden death. I thought maybe she used Quinn's cell phone to call me and his new number wasn't programmed into my cell. That would explain why the number didn't come up. However, when I answered the cell I heard static, then silence, then it sounded like someone hung up the receiver. I checked the cell phone's history of incoming calls but no numbers appeared. I thought this was strange because usually a number will appear, even if the display says UNKNOWN. It just usually means that the number is from an outside phone number and is not programmed into my phone. Then I would be able to click on the number and it would redial the person who called me. In this case, there were only the words UNKNOWN without any number. I thought the incident was strange, but I soon forgot about it.

Hours later my friend Jenna, called me and told me about a weird thing that happened to her and Quinn on the way to the airport. She said they were on their way to pick up Quinn's daughter, when the car radio blasted on and off really loud. Quinn doesn't listen to music very loud so he felt like his son was trying to get his attention and perhaps send him a message. I found out later that this happened around the same time that I received the strange phone call.

Four days later, the cell phone rang again, with the display reading the words UNKNOWN. I answered and heard static, then silence, then someone hang up. Once again I checked the history of incoming calls but there was no number.

About a month later, I was getting ready to go to a concert. I couldn't find the tickets anywhere in the house. I spent 2 ½ hours looking for the tickets but I never found them. I know I put them on the bookshelf on top of my other concert tickets. I only had them for a week. So I knew where I put them. They seemed to vanish into thin air.

Four days later, my friend Val, found them. They were sticking slightly out from under my stereo. I felt a slight chill because I knew I did not put them there. The bookshelf is on the other side of my room. There is no way they could have fallen there. Someone would have had to place them there. Was Quinn's son, Paul, trying to get my attention? He knew I was interested in the paranormal and would believe that his spirit may still be lingering around trying to make contact. Perhaps he was trying to relay a message.

Another strange thing that happened to me was that I had a dream about Paul, and he was trying to tell me something. When I woke up, I couldn't remember what the message was. I thought it was odd that I dreamt about him because I didn't know him very well and I wasn't thinking about him at the time.

A few days later my friend Jenna said that when Quinn was home alone and thinking about his son Paul, a strange thing happened. He was sad and feeling depressed and then he heard the stereo blast on and off very loud. Then the lights in the garage flickered on and off.

I then asked Jenna when the incident occurred. I figured out it was the same night that I had dreamt about Paul. This was about a day or two before Quinn's birthday. Was Paul trying to wish his father a happy birthday? Turning on and off the electrical appliances could be a way that he may be able to contact Quinn and get his attention. After all he still may have some unfinished business. He never got to say goodbye to his father or his daughter.

This is not the first time something like this has happened. Quinn's wife died three years earlier and there were similar occurrences.

One night, about 3:00am the living room stereo blasted on and off very loudly waking up Quinn. He ran into the living room checking to see what was going on and realized the stereo was turned completely off and the room was silent. He went back to bed and didn't hear another sound the rest of the night.

I used to clean his house and I would go there when no one was home. I would sometimes feel a presence in his bedroom. It seemed the strongest near the left side of the bed near the window and the bookcase. It didn't feel scary or threatening, just like someone was there watching me. Quinn had a big armchair in that area for awhile. One day I came to clean and the chair was gone. I found out that he had moved it upstairs. The room felt different and I didn't sense the feeling of being watched anymore.

This made me realize that maybe the chair was associated with the presence. When I inquired about the chair, Quinn said it was his wife's chair. She was the one that would always use it. Could it be part of her energy was left behind in one of her possessions? This has been known to happen in some cases.

Quinn's daughter was visiting during the holidays last year. That night she slept in his bedroom. She woke up in the middle of the night because she heard someone walk into the bedroom, go into the bathroom, and slam the door. She thought it was Quinn, so she just fell back to sleep. The next morning, she asked him, if he went into the bathroom during the night. He acted surprised. He said he was sleeping upstairs in the spare bedroom and didn't wake up at all in the middle of the night. He also said there is a bathroom upstairs so why would he walk downstairs and use that bathroom when there was another one only a few feet from where he was sleeping.

This incident happened around the time Quinn was having a memorial party for his wife.

I have gone to his house when no one is there and have taken many pictures and EVP recordings. I didn't get any evidence of a haunting, but that doesn't mean that there wasn't anything there. It could just mean the spirit isn't strong enough to appear or that it may choose not to. In both cases, the spirits, if any, could be Quinn's deceased wife and son.

Sometimes, when the grieving person is under extreme stress or sadness, the spirit may only appear to them or another family member. The purpose is to try to ease their grief and pain and reassure them that they are ok and that everything will be alright. The spirit may also be lingering around and try to make contact so that they can say goodbye. This can be done in a dream, or the spirit may try to move an object to get attention such as controlling electrical devices like cell phones, radios, lights, etc.

During the writing of this book, I was reading a similar story about the dead trying to contact the living through electronic devices. This particular story I happen to be reading coincidently a few days after Paul passed away. Then I remembered the cell phone incident that I had. It just made me believe more that Paul was trying to contact me or Quinn to explain about his sudden tragic death.

We still don't know what exactly happened that night. I also believe that Paul was trying to contact Quinn on his birthday. I think he may still be lingering around. However, I think his wife has moved on and passed over to the other side. His house feels different then it did a year ago. When you walk into the bedroom, I don't feel that strong presence anymore. I'm sure his wife has watched over him for awhile, but now she sees that he is doing better. He still has people who love and care about him. He is not alone. I think that may have been the reason why she stayed behind, but now she has no need to.

I feel that Paul may still be lingering around and only makes contact when his father is under extreme stress. I hope he finds some peace and moves on to a higher spiritual plane.

A few weeks before the 1 year anniversary of Paul's death, some strange occurrences started happening again at Quinn's house.

I think this was also because Paul's daughter was coming to visit her grandfather, Quinn. This is the last place that Paul's daughter lived before he passed away. I think he was trying to visit her there.

The first weird thing that happened occurred at Jenna's house. Her friend from Pennsylvania was visiting and staying in the spare room. This is the same room that I used to live in.

Jenna went to check in on her friend. She noticed her friend had fallen asleep with a baseball cap next to her head. When her friend woke up, Jenna asked her why did she have that hat? Her friend replied, "I don't know, I thought you put it there." They both shrugged it off until the next day.

Jenna's friend said that the towel bar came off the wall and fell on the bathroom floor. The strange thing was that it was not loose. She had to unscrew the remaining pieces that where still in the wall in order to put the towel bar back up. Then when Jenna walked into another room next to the bathroom, she saw a red baseball cap lying in the middle of the floor. There was no way that it could have ended up there unless someone put it there. All her hats were hanging on hooks behind the door, which was firmly pressed against the wall.

The next day, we had a gathering at Quinn's house. Jenna's sister came over and told us she had a weird experience the night before. She fell asleep on the couch and suddenly woke up around

11:30pm. In the corner of her eye, she saw a misty figure walk into the kitchen and then disappear. She has lived there for over 30 years and she has never seen anything like that before. This happened around the same time Jenna saw the baseball cap on her floor.

Just as they were telling me the story, Jenna's sister said she could smell nail polish remover. I had brought a small bag over with nail products inside. I thought the bottle probably fell out of the bag and spilled out all over the floor. However, when I went to clean it up, I noticed my bag was sitting upright on the chair. Inside was the bottle of nail polish remover, standing up straight and completely empty. It wasn't even knocked over. I was amazed. How could it have leaked out without falling? It was if someone opened it, spilled it out, and then placed it neatly back into my bag.

It seemed to me that someone was trying to get our attention. I think it was Paul, letting us know he was there and probably was excited his daughter was coming to visit.

The last weird incident that happened was when his daughter arrived.

Jenna had just brought her to Quinn's house. Everyone was gathered in the living room.

All of a sudden, Paul's daughter heard what sounded like an electronic voice of a toy say hello. She turned around and asked Jenna where the sound was coming from. Jenna replied "I have no idea." She was shocked. Everyone else in the room heard the voice also. However, their was no toy to be found.

I believe this was Paul trying to make some sort of contact with his daughter. He was doing whatever he could do to make his presence known.

SECTION III

Ghost Tours & My Own Investigations

PENNSYLVANIA

GETTYSBURG
2005

DEVILS DEN

I went to scout out haunted places to photograph in Gettysburg, Pennsylvania in August of 2005. I attended a couple of ghost tours the two nights that I was there.

Upon arriving, there was a very disgusting odor in the air. It smelled like a mixture of decay, fire, gunpowder, and rotten corn. It was very unusual. I've never experienced a smell like that before; it seemed to linger in the air most of the night.

There have been many odors accompanied with hauntings. During the bloody three day battle of 1863, 51,000 casualties and 5,000 horses died in these fields. The bodies were strewn out all over the battlefield, rotting in the heat. There was an overwhelming stench in the air of rotting corpses and carcasses. Many women in the town made sachets to help disguise the smell of the dead soldiers.

Some of the bodies were dropped into the crevices of rocks at Devils Den. The odor near this area became so putrid that the soldiers had to bury these bodies elsewhere. In order to do this, they had to pierce the torsos of the bodies and try to lift them from between these rocks and beneath the ground where they were imbedded. The bodies were decaying rapidly in the hot July sun. As they were being lifted, arms, legs, and flesh oozed off the corpses. Many body parts were left behind and slowly seeped into the ground.

There have been numerous sightings of wandering soldiers in this area. Perhaps the souls of these men are not at rest since they never received a proper burial. Parts of their bodies still remain intact in the earth. This is why I believe this area is so haunted. Everyone's bodies are made up of electrical impulses. There is an electromagnetic field around us at all times. When a person dies, sometimes this electricity or energy is released and trapped in our environment. This residual energy is what ghost hunters try to read with their EMF detectors. This validates that there is a presence in this area. Usually, that's when they try to take pictures or record this phenomenon.

This is where I am very intuitive. I can feel a presence without using and EMF detector. I felt a strong sense of physical pain and sadness when I climbed the rocks at Devils Den.

Energy sometimes can be transferred into objects. Hundreds of soldiers met their tragic demise at Devil's Den. The abundance of electricity there was imprinted in the boulders, much like a fossil. These huge rocks could be conductors for these electrical impulses. Therefore, the spirits are able to materialize by drawing the energy off of these boulders. This could be why there are so many sightings, even during the daytime.

I drove through the battlefield the next day. Although I didn't capture anything on film, I felt like I was experiencing something truly paranormal. An overwhelming feeling of sadness and gloom hung over me. My body felt very weak and tired. It almost felt like something was draining my life force. I felt like I was lying in a trench bleeding to death. I felt helpless and alone. I imagine this is what the soldiers must have been feeling at the time of their death.

MASS BURIAL SITES

Initially, the men who were killed at Gettysburg, were buried where they fell. Bodies were gathered into central burial locations. Long trenches were dug; bodies rolled in, and covered with a thin layer of dirt. Often shallow single graves were dug, the body placed in the pit and covered with just enough soil to dissuade scavengers. No attempts of embalming the bodies were made.

Identification was sketchy since there were no government issued "dog-tags". Maps of burial sites were made only by caring comrades who knew the family of the deceased. They thought the family would want the bodies of the soldiers for a proper burial. About 3,320 bodies were shipped to the southern states. Estimates of between a few hundred and over a thousand "missing bodies" is as close as anyone could get to the actual number of soldiers still buried on the battlefield. Bones and fragments of clothing are still being found into the new century. This could be why the battlefield is still haunted. The spirits of the dead are not at rest since their bodies are scattered throughout the battlefield. The never received a formal burial.

SCHOOLHOUSE ON HIGH STREET

Gettysburg, Pennsylvania was one of the most intriguing haunted places that I have been too. The whole town, not just the battlefield is haunted. A lot of the shops, and restaurants as well as residential houses seem to have paranormal activity. This is because the shops and restaurants were houses at one time where many wounded soldiers have died. There were so many injuries during the battle of Gettysburg but not enough hospitals or doctors to tend to these soldiers. The overflow of the wounded soldiers would be brought to certain homes, schools, or churches for medical treatment.

When I attended a walking ghost tour in August of 2005, I took many pictures. Almost every haunted place that I photographed, something strange appeared in the picture.

One night while on the tour, I saw an apparition of a Union soldier. It was so brief, I couldn't believe my eyes, it happened within seconds.

The tour guide was telling a story, and I was focusing on him. Then out of the corner of my peripheral vision, I saw a flash go by behind him. I didn't say anything because I wasn't sure if my mind was playing tricks on me or did I really see something. I saw only a lower torso and legs of a man walking up the road. I could only see from the waist down. His whole upper body, shoulders, arms, and face were invisible. I could see part of the soldier's blue jacket, a stripe down the side of his pants, and tall boots. The apparition would disappear and then reappear and then vanish completely within seconds. It seemed to be walking very quickly. It was incredible.

I also saw a lot of haunted houses that night, especially on High street, one of the most haunted streets in Gettysburg. On this street, many gruesome deaths occurred.

The Adams County Housing Authority on 59 East High Street at one time was a schoolhouse. It has a bloody history. This school was turned into a hospital for wounded soldiers. This is where many amputations were performed. There were so many, that the doctors would throw various body parts such as arms and legs, out the window from the third floor. The body parts would accumulate and there would be piles stacked up to the second story windows. After awhile, the parts began to rot and a horrible stench invaded the area.

The soldiers had to dig trenches on the side of the building in order to bury this gruesome sight. Sometimes the overflow of body parts was so abundant that they would have to burn the stacked up piles in a huge bonfire.

Eventually, these bodies had to be dug up. They were relocated and buried in a more permanent gravesite.

The area where these unfortunate souls have once laid is now paved over into a parking lot.

On several ghost tours, people have witnessed hearing screams of agony coming from the building as well as seeing an apparition of a soldier walking through the walls on the third floor.

This perhaps is the spirits of the slain soldiers who have died under the harshest conditions.

I have photographed this building two days in a row. In both pictures that I took, vortexes and orbs appeared. The paranormal activity seems to be concentrated in the front of the building where the amputated body parts were stacked up. There also appears to be a bright light surrounding the window where an apparition has been seen.

The Adams County Housing Authority
"The Old Schoolhouse" Gettysburg, Pa. 8/2005
(Day One)

The Adams County Housing Authority
"The Old Schoolhouse" Gettysburg, Pa. 8/2005
(Day Two)

GRIEVING STATUE

Another eerie place on High Street is behind the haunted schoolhouse. There is a cemetery here that once housed a statue of a lady sitting on a bench. The legend says that a couple were to be married in the nearby church but as the wedding day approached the groom never showed. The bride was jilted at the altar. The woman was so heartbroken that she didn't eat or sleep for weeks. She got very sick and died shortly after this tragic episode. Her family commissioned a statue in her honor. The memorial was the likeness of her sitting on a bench with her arms outstretched. This represented her lost love. This statue looked very peculiar, and as word of mouth got around people would come to look at this sad memorial.

Unfortunately, it became popular among the college students. The fraternities started a hazing tradition where they would send a new pledge to this statue. The chosen one would have to sit in the arms of the statue over night, until someone returned to him in the morning.

One time upon returning, the frat brother started calling out the name of the kid sleeping on the statue. There was no response. So he proceeded to shake him in order to wake him up. After several failed attempts he finally realized the kid was not moving. He was dead.

The coroner arrived to inspect the body. The police couldn't find any signs of foul play. The body was taken away for an autopsy. It was difficult to find the cause of death. It was concluded that the college student died of exposure. This was very unusual because it was warm that night. There wasn't any frostbite found on the body. The only thing that was strange was the marks found on his neck. The imprints looked like finger marks around his throat, almost as if he was strangled. This theory however was never proven.

Upon further investigation, ironically this college student was related to the man who jilted the woman at the altar. He was the grandson. Did the spirit of the bride possess the statue? Did she get her final revenge by killing him? Or was this just pure coincidence? This is something to ponder as you walk the streets of Gettysburg hoping to get a glimpse of our past history.

THE CHURCH ON HIGH STREET

The Trinity United Church of Christ on South Stratton Street and High Street was the church where the couple was to be married. It also has a morbid history.

This is located down the street on the same side as the haunted cemetery with the statue. This church housed many casualties of war. The bodies of the soldiers were laid out on the pews, since there were not enough beds in the hospitals. Holes had to be drilled in the benches to let the blood drain to the floor. So much blood accumulated on the floor that additional holes had to be drilled to let the blood drain down further into the ground. Many people have experienced eerie sounds and shadows at night while walking past this area where the church still remains. My photo shows some vortexes coming out of this building. Could this be the energy that the soldiers left behind? Perhaps, this imprint remained so that they would not be forgotten.

The Trinity United Church of Christ
Gettysburg, Pa 8/2005

THE OLD JAIL ON HIGH STREET

Across the street from the schoolhouse, is a building that was once The Adams County Prison. This is said to be haunted by Gus, he is a friendly spirit who was either a former inmate or the prison's cook. He passed away many years ago. Sometimes the guards and prisoners would smell the aromas of cooking in the middle of the night. This was strange because they would be the only people in the jail at the time.

This building is now a motor- vehicle's office. There was a couple who had a chilling experience here, while waiting for a parking ticket to be paid.

While the woman was paying the parking ticket, her husband was waiting for her in the car. When he looked in the rear view mirror, he saw a soldier sitting in the backseat. He was so alarmed that he drove around the block hoping that the soldier would disappear, which he did. When his wife returned, he told her his experience but she didn't believe him.

A few weeks later, the couple had to pay another parking ticket. This time the wife decided to wait in the car. It was parked at the same spot as the previous time. This was across the street in front of the old haunted schoolhouse. Once again, the soldier appeared. The woman noticed him in the rearview mirror, sitting in the backseat. He remained silent and just stared ahead. The wife also drove around the block a few times until he disappeared. They both couldn't believe this happened twice. It scared them so much that they made sure not to get another ticket again.

During the Civil War, the ambulances looked like black trucks with black tarp roofs. The wounded soldiers would jump in the back of these vehicles. Perhaps, the ghost thought their car was an ambulance. So not only the battlefield and the houses are haunted but also the streets of Gettysburg have many wandering spirits trying to find their way home. Almost the whole town of Gettysburg was once a battlefield. Some modern buildings are built on old burial grounds where soldiers have died. With so much death and suffering no wonder why spirits linger there.

I photographed this building two days in a row. On both days, the pictures reveal L-shaped vortexes appearing in the windows. On the second night, there are more intense vortexes in front of the building coming from the lower floor.

Adams County Prison
Gettysburg, Pa. 8/2005
(L-shaped vortexes)
Day One

Adams County Prison
Gettysburg, Pa. 8/2005
(Intense Vortexes)
Day Two

TWIN SYCAMORES

Across the street from the Farnsworth House is a building that I photographed on the ghost tour. It is a small Bed & Breakfast called "Twin Sycamores" located on Baltimore & Lefever Street. There were many sharpshooters stationed in this house during the war. They would fire their rifles towards the battlefield, which is now a high school. There have been many sightings of a ghostly soldier roaming the grounds of this area. He has been described as a young man with half of his face blown off due to a gunshot wound. He walks back and forth from Twin Sycamores to the park across the street. A man reported seeing a soldier running straight at him, then shouting as if he was in combat and then he disappeared.

The building is named after the two huge Sycamore trees that are on the property. President Abraham Lincoln stopped at this spot to admire these two beautiful trees.

Vortexes appear in the photo where the apparition of the soldier has been seen.

Twin Sycamores
Gettysburg, Pa. 8/2005

Twin Sycamores
Gettysburg, Pa. 8/2005

THE WOODEN BRIDGE

Behind Twin Sycamores is a high school. There was once a wooden foot bridge located on the property of the school. It was above a stream that is no longer there. The landscape has changed dramatically in the last 100 years. Most of the trees and houses in Gettysburg were not there during the Civil War. The majority of the town is built over the battlefield. This is why there are so many strange occurrences throughout the town. Many wounded soldiers fell into this trench under the bridge to hide during the battle. They were wounded so badly they became weak and couldn't get out. They tried to cling on to the bridge and pull themselves out. It rained heavily on July 3rd and July 4th. This stream flooded and many soldiers drown in this ditch. Others died slowly of infected wounds.

Over the years, there has been scratch marks seen imbedded in the wooden handrails of the bridge. They would keep reappearing after being sanded down and repainted. Some people have claimed to feel hands grabbing their feet by unseen forces as they walk over this bridge and the surrounding area. Moans and cries of pain and agony have been heard late at night. These odd occurrences happened so often that eventually the bridge was torn down and the hole was filled in and paved over. This part of the road was bought by a school and the area was made into a parking lot. I photographed this paved area in total darkness and received some startling results. There are some weird lines that showed up in the picture, just like the ones that have taken at other haunted sites. Could this be the spirits of the soldiers who died there? I think so. We are naïve to think that we are the only ones in our vast universe.

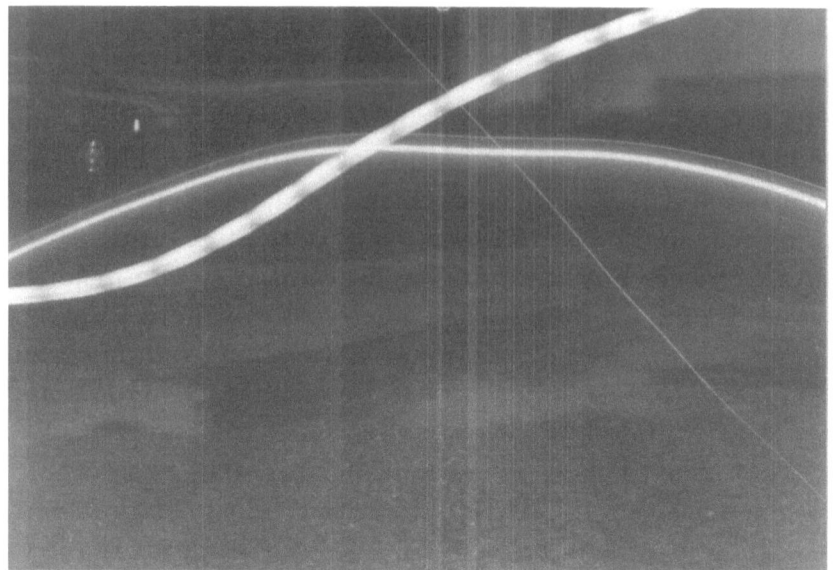

Parking lot behind the school (Once a wooden foot bridge)
Gettysburg, Pa 8/2005

THE BASEMENT OF THE
FARNSWORTH HOUSE

The Farnsworth House has a morbid history of death and violence. There are many claims that the house is inhabited by fourteen ghosts. Currently, it is a Bed and Breakfast which has a restaurant and tavern. Originally, during the war of Gettysburg, it housed sharpshooters in the upstairs attic. There are one hundred and fifty bullet holes in the wall, still reminiscent of the war. They are visible on the side of the house near the entrance of the tavern. There are various entities that dwell in the basement of the Farnsworth House. Many dead bodies have been found in the basement, after the war.

A beheaded soldier was found lying dead at the bottom of the steps. Another soldier's body was found face down in the corner of the cellar. A third soldier was shot in the neck. His blood splattered and sprayed the wall of the basement.

There are some nice spirits as well as evil spirits trapped in this domain. One is a woman who is drawn to mothers and caretakers. She has been known to have a healing touch. People who have visited the Farnsworth House, have miracously been healed of certain ailments after being touched by her icy hands.

Another friendly spirit is a prankster. It is believed to be a spirit of a little boy. Some people claim that their shoe laces have been tied together, while they were sitting down. They tried to get up but couldn't. Toys appear and disappear near the small shrine dedicated to this spirit. This is most likely the ghost of a boy who was accidentally trampled by a horse in front of the Farnsworth House. He was brought inside and died shortly afterwards in one of the bedrooms.

There is also an evil presence that does not like women. When his name is mentioned, usually it stirs him up and he causes havoc. This ghost has been known to be called "Walter". His name was mentioned the night we were there, and some people have claimed to have seen him. When I went upstairs into the attic, I had a hair-raising experience. The door suddenly opened as my friend and I were listening to the tour guide. It creaked and moved slowly, opening only halfway. We both jumped and looked at each other, then at the tour guide. He shut the door, but it kept opening. He had to put a chair in front of the door to stop it. This incident was a little scary because it happened shortly after the ghost of "Walter" was mentioned. He has been known to roam the attic that we were sitting in. Luckily, that was the only experience that we had upstairs.

The next area that we went to was the basement of the Farnsworth Inn. Another tour guide was there talking about the tragic deaths that have occurred there over the years. He uses divining rods in order to track the existence of ghosts. Modern ghost hunters today use more electronic devices such as EMF detectors to experience the same effect.

Divining rods have been used since ancient times. Typically, they are used for finding underground water, oil, or mineral resources. They measure energy patterns that naturally occur. However, they are also used in some occult practices such as dowsing. This is a form of divination. The rods in this case, are used to measure energy from unseen forces, such as ghosts. It can pick up their energy when they are around.

Everyone has an aura, or energy that surrounds our physical bodies. As this energy or light radiates, sometimes it's released into the air. The Divining rod can pick up or read this energy. Ghosts also emit energy or vibrations. Some people, like myself, are sensitive to these vibrations or energy. I can sense if a ghost is present.

Divining rods can be used to help develop our natural physic abilities. They usually are "L" shaped wire rods made of brass. Brass is used because it doesn't interfere with the earth's magnetic field. It is a more accurate reading. The rods cross over one another marking an "X", when an object is found. When using them, you have to hold one in each hand.

I had a spine-tingling encounter using divining rods in the basement Of the Farnsworth House in Gettysburg, Pennsylvania. There was a Storyteller in the basement, talking about the hauntings that occur regularly in the house. He had a pair of handmade divining rods. After his stories were told, he brought out the rods. He said he used these to pick up energy or vibrations left by the spirits.

To begin, you take a rod in each hand, holding them straight out from your body and parallel to the ground. If someone walks towards you, the rods go completely backwards towards your arms and shoulders. When someone walks away from you, they go back in front of you. Sometimes they lean to the right or the left.

When I picked up the rods, they were flinging all over the place. They were going backwards, hitting my upper arms. I could feel the energy. It felt overwhelming, like I was picking up multiple spirits standing in front of me. Some of the emotions I felt were sad, lonely, and angry. I also sensed an evil presence, perhaps it was Walter, the resident ghost of the hotel. I suddenly felt uncomfortable, and I wanted to leave.

When my friend and her mother picked up the rods, they felt content. They must have contacted only the good spirits. At one point, the rods Criss-crossed and formed an "x" under my friend's neck. She felt that the spirit liked her and was trying to protect her from the other evil spirits that linger in the house. Her mother had a similar experience. She felt happy, positive, and upbeat. Her rods pointed towards a door of a room that ghosts have been known to inhabit. They both believe that they encountered either the friendly old lady or the spirit of the playful boy.

I think I'm the only one who sensed the evil lurking in the catacombs behind the door.

I have taken extraordinary pictures of the Farnsworth House. Powerful vortexes appear outside the house and directly in front of me. These lights of energy are possibly from the spirits that reside within.

The Farnsworth House
Gettysburg, Pa. 8/2005

The Farnsworth House
Gettysburg, Pa. 8/2005

JENNIE WADE HOUSE

Mary Virginia Wade was the only civilian that was killed during the battle of Gettysburg. She was baking bread in the kitchen when a stray Confederate bullet penetrated two doors and struck her in the back. The bullet passed through her heart, killing her instantly. She had left her mothers home to stay at her sister's hoping to escape from the war. Unfortunately, this house ended up in the center of the battle. This is where she was killed.

Jennie Wade was engaged to Jack Skelley. They both had a mutual friend named Wesley Culp. Jack and Wesley went off to the war, while Jennie retreated to her sister's house. Jack wrote a letter to Jennie and asked if Wesley could deliver it to her. The message however, was never delivered. Wesley died while fighting on his family's property near Culps Hill. Jennie never received the letter, she died on July 3rd an hour later after the letter was written. Jack died 9 days after Jennie, never knowing whether the message was delivered.

The Jennie Wade House is now a museum which is the oldest in Gettysburg. It was founded in 1904. There is a statue of Jennie Wade in front of the house. I took pictures here at night and some strange lines showed up around this monument. I also photographed the door where the stray bullet went through. You can still see the hole where the bullet penetrated. An eerie glowing light appeared in my picture. It is surrounding the doorway. There have been many strange occurrences in this house. Objects have been moved around, or appear out of nowhere. Many of the staff who worked there claimed to have seen shadows, heard voices, and cold spots were often felt throughout the house. Camera batteries have been drained when people have tried to photograph this museum.

Most of the voices have been reported, coming from the second floor bedroom. One eerie incident that happened, was an employee heard what sounded like a group of people coming out of the brick wall; walk down the stairs and out the back door. This could possibly be the ghosts of the soldiers who carried Jennie Wade's body through the two homes and into the cellar on the south side of the building. It is rumored that her body was buried in the basement under the dirt floor. I certainly felt a strong presence there when I entered the gift shop to purchase the tickets for the tour.

When I developed the pictures very prominent vortexes appeared in the front of the house. As I looked closer, I realized an image of a woman's face appears in the right side of the photo. Could this be Jennie Wade still waiting for Jack to return?

Can the hauntings of the Jennie Wade House be attributed to the spirits of Jennie, Jack, and Wes trying to find each other? Could they have finally reunited in death? Well, that's something to ponder if you ever get a chance to visit this historical museum.

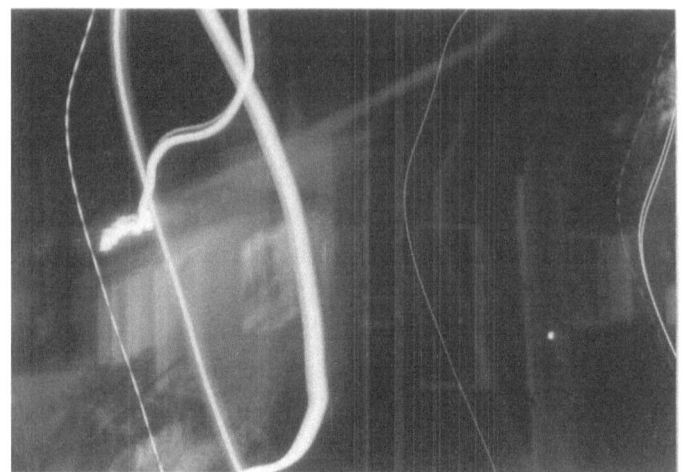

The Jennie Wade House
Gettysburg, Pa. 8/2005
(Image appears in right hand corner)

The famous door to the Jennie Wade House Gettysburg, Pa. 8/2005
(Strange light surrounding the door)

HAUNTED BATTLEFIELD

The next photo was taken in one of the areas of the battlefield. It wasn't near a monument or anything at all. It was pitch dark that night on August 26, 2005. My friend and I had just come from a ghost tour and decided to take a ride to the battlefield. Unfortunately, this area was closed, so I couldn't go in and walk around.

It felt like something or someone was drawing me to this particular spot. I decided to snap a picture of the field in the dark to see if we could get anything.

When this picture was taken, a flash like fireworks seemed to go off in front of the camera and this photo was the result. These vortexes represent spirits trying to manifest themselves. I think the red signifies a violent death. This could be the very spot where soldiers were gunned down and killed. They are still roaming the battlefields. I think the spirits drained all the energy in my camera in order to appear this way. After this photo was taken, the battery in my camera was totally drained and I wasn't able to take anymore pictures of this area.

Gettysburg Battlefield
Gettysburg, Pa. 8/2005

Finally, we got tired and decided to drive home. As we approached the highway, there appeared to be something huge lying in the middle of the road. It looked like a dead body in a very large burlap bag. I immediately thought it was the shape and size of a very tall soldier.

I couldn't believe my eyes. I had to look a few times in order to see what it was. We almost hit it with the car that night. My friend swerved out of the way very quickly so we wouldn't run it over. We were laughing, but it was actually pretty scary. We had just seen some weird things on the ghost tour that night. I didn't know if my mind was playing tricks on me. However, my friend had also seen it so I know it was definitely something. We didn't stop to see what it was; we just kept driving to get away from it. We never did find out what it was. I thought it was probably a ghostly vision of the past reminding us what happened during the bloody three day battle. All I know is that I was happy to leave Gettysburg that night.

MILFORD
2006

THE COLUMNS

On February 12, 2006, I was running around taking pictures of the Milford Jail and Theatre, I also went to photograph a building called the Columns located at 608 Broad Street in Milford, Pennsylvania. This is the home of the Pike County Historical Society. This is also where the famous Lincoln Flag is on display.

As I approached the building, I walked up the wooden stairs and entered the wide doors of this beautiful Victorian house. As you walk to the right, a huge room opens up. This is where the Lincoln flag is located. The reason why it is so famous is because this is the flag that was placed under President's Lincoln's head after he had been shot. The bloodstains are very visible as you look closely at the flag.

Abraham Lincoln was shot by John Wilkes Booth on April 14, 1865. This Flag had been draped over the balustrade at Ford's Theatre. A part-time stage manager named Thomas Gourlay placed the flag under Lincoln's head after he was shot. The President was then moved across the street to the Peterson House. The flag was returned to Gourlay who then gave it to his daughter. It was then passed down through the family. Eventually, in 1954 the flag was given to the Pike County Historical Society. It still remains in their possession.

There have been many debates whether this flag is authentic. Due to extensive research, it was confirmed that this is the flag that Abraham Lincoln rested his head upon.

Some people believe Lincoln had psychic abilities. He had claimed to foresee his own murder in his dreams. He dreamt that he saw himself lying in a coffin dead. This was only ten days prior to his assassination. One of his bodyguards named W.H. Crook, also had a similar dream and begged Lincoln not to attend Fords Theatre that fateful night. He had a feeling of impending doom was about to occur.

There have been many indications that Abraham Lincoln is a ghost. He has been sited in the White House where he was the President, Springfield Illinois where he was buried and Gettysburg, Pennsylvania where he addressed his famous speech. He has also been seen roaming the battlefield.

In 2006, I think I had a special connection with Lincoln. It seemed that everywhere I looked I would see a sign of his presence. He was mentioned in almost everything I read or looked at. He was on posters, paintings, billboards, in commercials, on the radio, in the movies, bookstores, etc. It seemed like he was following me trying to tell me something.

It all started when I went on a ghost tour in Gettysburg, Pennsylvania. I stopped in front of a huge oak tree admiring its beauty. The tour guide said that this is the famous tree that Lincoln stopped in front of to gather his thoughts. Every time he was in Gettysburg he would stop at this area to admire the enormous tree. This is located next to Twin Sycamores. After I heard this, the chain of events began.

The following year, I returned to Gettysburg to attend another ghost Tour of the Soldiers Museum, which was an orphanage at one time. I couldn't find parking on the street. After driving around the block a few times, I happened to find a spot across the street from The Farnsworth House. When I got out of the car to put money in the meter, I glanced over at an enormous tree. I then realized I was parked next to the same tree that Lincoln and I both admired. Was his ghost drawing me back to this spot for some reason? Sometimes a ghost can attach to a person. They try to get your attention so they can give you a message or they want you to help them in some way. I never did figure out why the strange events kept happening to me.

The next year the weird signs started to appear again. Everywhere I looked, there was references pertaining to Lincoln. I felt like he was trying to tell me something. This feeling got stronger as it approached Presidents Day.

That weekend my friend Val was driving and I was in the passenger seat. We were traveling back home from East Stroudsburg, Pennsylvania. We had been shopping all day. I glanced over to my right side and I saw a billboard with Lincoln's face on it. I made a joke about him following me, and we both laughed. Then I felt a hand grab my left knee. It felt like someone squeezed my knee tight and then it felt all tingly. It startled me so bad I nearly jumped out of my seat.

Then I shouted, "Please Lincoln leave me alone" "I know you are here and I believe in you, but you are scaring me so please don't bother me anymore". Shortly after this happened all the signs and references to Lincoln stopped. I didn't see or hear anything about him for a year.

I thought this was because I moved from Shohola, Pennsylvania to Albuquerque, New Mexico. But then it started up again. Everywhere I looked he was around. Even stranger yet, is that when I was writing this story, I glanced down at the calendar and realized that tomorrow was Lincoln's birthday. How strange it was to be writing this story almost exactly 2years later from the time I took those photos. Another weird thing that happened to me the same day was when I was reading a ghost book. The introduction mentioned that President Lincoln still walks the earth.

This is one of the reasons why I wanted to come to the Columns and photograph it. Since his flag was on display I thought maybe I could catch a glimpse of his ghost. After all, his blood and DNA are imprinted in the flag. I decided to take pictures at night, on his birthday, which was also during a full moon. It was a perfect night with all the right conditions. I took 35mm pictures as well as digital.

I developed the film and saw some paranormal activity in the photos. In one picture there is an orb hovering around the front of the building. In another there is an eerie green light illuminating from the same window near the front of the Columns. Behind that window is where the Lincoln flag is displayed.

Is this possibly Lincoln? Is his ghost still lingering around the Columns? Could he just be visiting since his ghost has been known to roam through the White House hallways and Gettysburg battlefields? Is he still walking this earth trying to protect our country? Perhaps he has unfinished business to take care of that he never had a chance to do when he was President since his life was ended so abruptly. I would like to think he is a great savior or angel looking down and watching over me, trying to guide me through the trials and tribulations of this world.

The Columns
Milford, Pa. 2/2006
(Green light and mist surrounds the front porch)

HARFORD INN

The Harford Inn is located on 401 East Hartford Street in Milford, Pennsylvania. This 270 year old building now sits vacant in the heart of town. It is a three story Colonial house that was built in 1733. The house has seven rooms in addition to the carriage house, which has two floors. There is a small building outside that was once an outhouse. It was built to accommodate three adults and one child. It is now used as a shed.

The upstairs windows of the Inn are shaped like half moons. This was designed so that the settlers could easily shoot a rifle out the window to defend themselves against the invading Indians. It is believed the area near the back shed was part of the Underground Railroad. The Schuylkill Creek runs behind this house. It was a quick escape route for slaves to travel and hide.

In the 1800's, an estimated 100,000 enslaved people sought freedom through the Underground Railroad. This term was used to describe the secret routes that enslaved men, women, and children to gain their freedom. It had several branches and extended from the Deep South and Texas to states and territories where slavery had been prohibited. Many slaves kept moving until they reached Canada or Mexico. These two nations abolished slavery. Many slaves that escaped received help and protection from free Blacks, Whites, Native Americans and other slaves. They provided food and shelter along the way. This house was believed to be such a place.

In the 1940's a wealthy Westfall Oil & Fuel Company owner lived in this house. During the time Harry S Truman was president he had the White House renovated. The flooring was ripped up and some fireplaces were removed. They were put up for sale for $100 each. The wealthy owner of the Harford Inn purchased one of these fireplaces and it was installed downstairs.

The kitchen in the Harford Inn was once the home of the Pike County Dispatch, which is the local newspaper. A plumber found some Type letters underneath the floorboards when he was making some repairs on the pipes.

The Harford Inn was once a bed and breakfast run by manager Patricia Edwards from 1988-1997. I interviewed her and she told me about the Inn being haunted. She worked and lived there for 9 years. Strange things started to happen almost immediately after she moved in. There seemed to be activity on almost every floor of the house. The most activity seemed to be concentrated on the first floor where the dining room and living room are located.

One strange incident that she remembers happened between December 1987 and January 1988. Patricia was decorating for Christmas on the lower floor. She placed fake snow on the windowsills and the shelves. She also placed a ceramic plate on the shelf. This was very sentimental to her since her daughter made it for her as a present. She went into the other room for awhile and then returned to finish her decorating. When she came back, she noticed the plate had been moved. When she got closer to it she realized there were small handprints (like a child's) in the fake snow. She would put the plate back where it was originally, only to find it moved again and again. This occurred every half-hour. This continued to happen every time she moved the plate. It would get moved somewhere else. At this point she was convinced that the Inn was haunted. She got very angry and yelled at the unseen spirit. She had enough. She said "If you break that, I'm gonna kill you, my daughter made that for me." Since she saw those handprints she thought maybe this was a spirit of a child that only wanted to play. It was trying to get her attention. After this incident the activity ceased, at least for a little while. It started up again in December of 1990. The same activity occurred again.

Another odd thing was that this room always smelled like the aroma of heavy perfume with the scent of flowers. This seemed to indicate a female presence was around. Pat would also hear doors slamming above her and on the first floor, when there was no one around. A few times she even saw a black shadow go past her very quickly and then disappear.

Many guests staying on the second and third floors have complained about being woken up in the middle of the night by people talking loudly. It sounded like they were having a party in the other room. The following day, when they checked out, they asked who those obnoxious people were? To their surprise, they found out that no one was there the previous night except for them. Pat said she also heard these voices in the Queen Room, located on the 2nd floor.

Another eerie part of the building is the basement. It had a dirt floor. Anytime, anyone went downstairs into the basement it felt like someone was there watching you. The lights would turn on and off by themselves. The pilot light in the furnace would always go out. One time Pat called an electrician to check this out. He was down in the basement for a short time, and then he ran out of the building vowing never to come back. Something scared him but he never told her what he saw or heard. As he was leaving he mumbled something about the house being haunted.

There is also a shed behind this house, where Pat said she heard drumming and Indian chanting. The Schuylkill Creek runs behind this house into the Delaware River. The Lenni-Lenape Indians once heavily populated this area.

Pat showed me a picture that she had taken many years ago. It was a picture of the 2nd floor bedroom. When I looked closer, I noticed the image of a little girl peering into the window from the outside. There is no way she could have looked through the window, unless she was floating through mid-air. This window is two stories up from the ground. I asked Pat if I could make a copy of this photo for my book. She said yes, but she had not been able to find this picture since she showed it to me. That was about three years ago. It seemed to vanish into thin air just like the ghosts.

Eventually, the current Harford Inn's owner ran into some legal issues, and the Inn was closed for good. Pat went into retirement a little earlier then expected. She moved into another Inn, named the Pegasus Inn, located in Shohola, Pennsylvania. This was run by a couple of her friends she met while she was running the

Harford Inn. This time she was a resident rather then a manager. This Inn is also known to have some supernatural occurrences. Did Pat follow ghosts or did they seem to find her? They seem to cling to her caring, sympathetic nature.

I photographed the Harford Inn on February 13, 2006 I took pictures of the front of the Harford Inn and the shed in the back. In both pictures, I got the same paranormal activity. Thick heavy lines or streaks of light known as vortexes appeared in the pictures. They appeared to be red and green. Red usually indicates a violent death. I was amazed, because I just happen to take photos that night out of the blue. I did not plan to go there that night. I was driving home late from East Stroudsburg, Pennsylvania. I knew I would be passing by and I happen to have the camera with me. I'm usually never in town that late, so I thought it was a good chance to catch something paranormal. I just had a gut feeling to stop and take some pictures. I felt like something was luring me there. Usually when I have this feeling, I end up getting anomalies in the photos. I really believe I am intuitive to the paranormal. Sure enough, something did show up in the photos.

Shed next to the Harford Inn
Milford, Pa. 2/2006
(Vortexes in front of the shed)

The Harford Inn
Milford, Pa. 2/2006
(Vortexes in the right side of the photo)

MILFORD THEATRE

During my high school years, I heard stories that the Milford Theatre on 114 East Catherine Street was haunted. Strange sounds have been heard coming from the stage area behind the screen and near the dressing rooms on the basement level. Lights in the building would flicker on and off. Sometimes the film projector would stop and refuse to operate. There would be a sudden stillness and chill in the air. When you walked into the theatre an overwhelming presence could be felt staring at you. One time a person could be heard sneezing when there was only one employee in the theatre. These are some of the incidents that have been claimed according to a former manager, Joseph Edwards who was working there from 1988 to 1994. Milford Theatre is located in a historic Victorian village next to the Delaware River. It is about 75 miles west from New York City. The town of Milford, Pennsylvania attracts many local artists and film enthusiasts. The Annual Black Bear Film Festival is held here every third weekend of October. There are also free films and lectures during the festival.

The building is a little beat up, but it has its charm. The original interior and classic neon marquee is still intact. The seats are not as comfortable as modern stadium seating but they are maintained very well. It really gives you a feeling that you are back in time. An interesting thing about the seating is that there used to be little box seats on both sides of the theatre on the same level as the rest of the seats. Normally, box seats are up higher and closer to the stage. In 2003, the supporters of the Black Bear Film Festival purchased a new screen. This enabled them to run movies there.

The Milford Theatre was opened in the early twenties by Thomas Pitney. It was originally a silent movie house. The theatre's rigging curtains and doors were acquired from the 1939 New York World's Fair. Various people have operated it over the last several decades. In 1984, it was leased to the owners of the Forestburg, New York Playhouse. For one fall season, they put on several plays. The theatre has been shut down and re-opened many times over the years.

The dressing rooms were all on the basement level. It was very dank and chilly down there. Former employees, as well as actors, complained of feeling uncomfortable while being alone in the dressing rooms at night. They said it felt like someone was watching them. This is supposedly where an apparition of a man has been sighted. There is a rumor that an early producer or owner of the theater had hung himself from the fly loft for reasons unknown. This possibly took place in the 1920's or 1930's. It has never been confirmed. Could it be his spirit that haunts this old theatre?

On February 12 2006, I went to photograph this theatre. It was the same night I took pictures of the Milford Jail and the Columns. I already felt a little nervous when I jumped out of the car and told my friend to turn off the car's headlights. I wanted to get a picture of the theatre in complete darkness. I felt little uneasy snapping pictures that night. I could feel the energy in the air. The presence felt very strong as I approached the building. I could sense something was there. Sure enough my instincts were right. Some green vortexes appeared in my photograph in front of the building known as the Milford Theatre.

The Milford Theatre
Milford, Pa. 2/2/006
(Green vortexes on the right side)

OLD MILFORD JAIL

(OLD STONE COURTHOUSE)

I went to investigate the Old Milford Jail on Catherine Street on February 12, 2006. There was a full moon that evening so I was hoping to capture some paranormal activity in my photos. I have done this before and have been successful in this approach.

It was a perfect night to snoop around. There was no-one visible in town or on the streets. The small quaint town closes down early, usually by 5:00pm it is literally a ghost town.

Since it was February, the coldest month in rural Pennsylvania, there was a lot of ice and snow compacted in the ground. The temperature was in the low teens but it was a very clear, starry night.

My friend, Val and I arrived in town around 9:00pm and parked across the street from the jail. I wanted to be able to get a good shot of the whole building. If I was on the same side as the jail, it would have been too close to take a picture. We parked on the street next to the Tom Quick Inn & Restaurant. This building has also been rumored to have ghostly inhabitants. I took pictures of the Tom Quick Inn's doorway, porch, and side of the building but didn't capture anything unusual. The air seemed to be very still and quiet that night.

A strange thing happened to me when I was about to snap a picture of the jail, I almost fell forward into the snow. It felt like someone tripped me. I felt a quick pressure of air near my legs, and then I lunged forward but regained my balance. I quickly snapped a few photos. Then I moved closer to the jail, and it happened again just as I was about to take some side views of the jail. This made me feel a little uneasy. It was as if someone or something was preventing me from taking these photos. I kept thinking to myself, this ghost doesn't want me taking pictures. Then it occurred to me that this town was once heavily populated by the Lenni- Lenape Indian tribe. Indian ground is very sacred and they don't allow people to take pictures of their land.

I decided to get in the car and go home, since I was tripped twice. I was positive that I photographed something paranormal. Sure enough, when I developed the film there was something there. There were a lot of colorful green streaks called vortexes. This usually indicates paranormal activity. During a full moon there is always a higher chance of capturing some type of supernatural occurrence. I proved to myself that my intuition was accurate when I viewed the photographs. I could feel the energy in the air that night.

It was very hard to find any history about this old jail. I am not sure who haunts it, but I have my theories. One is that the jail is built on Lenni- Lenape Territory.

The tribe that settled in Milford was the Lenni-Lenape, which means "true people". They were also known as the Delaware Indians. The Delaware River runs through their territory. They are the original people of the mid-Atlantic area.

The British drove the Lenape Indians out of their homeland. Many Lenape Indians were relocated to Oklahoma. Their population is 16,000. There are still some small Lenape tribes living in Pennsylvania and New Jersey. They are not officially recognized as tribes by the United States. This means they do not have their own governmental system or reservation land. Today all Lenape Indians speak English.

The Lenape men were hunters. They used bows and arrows. They went hunting for deer, elk, turkeys, and small game. They caught fish in the rivers and outlets along the Delaware River. Sometimes they went to war to protect their families. Lenape warriors wielded heavy wooden war clubs and shields of moose hide and wood.

The women were farmers harvesting corn, squash, and beans. They did most of the childcare and the cooking. Both took part in storytelling, artwork, music, and traditional medicine. The chiefs were always men.

The Lenape lived in roundhouses called wigwams. The tribe used bark and dugout canoes to travel on the Delaware River and the East Coast. In the winter they used sleds and snowshoes to get around.

The Lenape men wore a beaded headband with a feather or two sticking out of it. Sometimes during ceremonies the chief would wear a headdress. They painted their faces with different colors and designs for different occasions. The men wore tattoos in an animal design. The men had Mohawks or shaved their heads completely except for a scalp lock in the middle. The women wore their hair in long braids.

I have a friend Patricia Edwards, who has lived in Milford for 15 years. She told me that in the 1980's, she heard stories of weird things going on in the cells. Some prison guards had reported hearing rattling of the bars in the cell, and footsteps walking the hallways when no one else was present. One time rain had fallen inside the cell, and it wasn't even raining outside. How could this possibly be explained? Rain shouldn't mysteriously appear from an unknown source. Indian tribes have performed rain-dancing ceremonies in order to provoke rainfall so their crops would be more abundant and ensure harvest protection. The dance was unique. Both men and women move in zigzag patterns, rather then dancing in a circle. The dances were primarily performed in the hot summer months like August. Rain dances vary for different tribes. Their legend and the specific steps have been passed down from generation to generation. So perhaps the Indian ghosts created this rain.

Tom Quick was known as the Indian Slayer or the Avenger of the Delaware. At one time he was friends with the Indian tribe that lived on the Delaware River. Tom Quick was born in Milford, Pennsylvania in 1734. His father Thomas Quick Sr. built a log cabin and his neighbors were the Indians. Tom Jr. became familiar with Indian language, engaged in many of their sports, hunted and fished with them and became an expert in the use of the rifle. This friendship with the Indians wouldn't last long.

The Indians were alarmed at the increasing demands and encroachments of the whites. They were afraid the whites would invade and take over their beloved homes and territory. They felt that steps were needed to be taken to prevent this from happening. The Indians devised a plan for the destruction of the entire white population. During this time, the Quicks noticed the change of behavior in the Indians and decided to no longer mingle with them.

One day when the Quicks were on the river, an Indian named Muswink shot and killed Toms father. At this moment, Tom Jr.

shouted that he would "swear eternal vengeance on the whole Indian race". He became "The Avenger of the Delaware". He killed many Indians at this time. He took refuge in the mountains and had only his gun for a companion. He eventually died of smallpox. The Indians dug up his remains and distributed them among the various tribes and gloated over them. It seems that Tom Quick had the last laugh because smallpox broke out and infected many of the Indians.

In 1899, Tom's bones were dug up and buried underneath a monument that was built in his honor. This monument has been very controversial. The remaining Lenape Indians have tried several times to have this monument taken down. They had a petition going around in 1999 asking the town council to have this monument covered, removed, or concealed out of sight. They stated that the monument is a constant horrific and racist reminder of the slaughter of innocent Lenape men, women, and children and/or other indigenous Indians. They felt that the monument evoked racist and bigoted feelings within the Borough of Milford and in the state of Pennsylvania. If it was removed, the memory of the killings would be lessened and mended. The Indians can begin the process of healing and move forward so that they can live in peace.

Tom Quick, was an Indian slayer who killed many Indian men, women, and children near the Delaware river. He invaded their land and seized their property. I believe this jail is located on their land. It could be the reason why it is haunted. Are the lost Lenape Indian souls still lingering around or it could be the lonely prisoners who have died in the cells. I couldn't find anything confirming the haunting but I did find an interesting story of someone who was imprisoned there.

In 1848, the bridge for the railroad over the Lackawaxen River in Pennsylvania was being built. The structure was 400 feet in length. There were 200 Irish railroad laborers as well as a number of local men working on this project. Of course, there were many fights among the local men and Irish during the construction of this bridge. One night a man was stabbed. His name was George Kays. He was a very peaceful and quiet man who never bothered anyone. The stabbing was premeditated and a very violent assault. The man who stabbed him was Patrick Callaghan. He was one of the Irish men on the bridge job.

The justice of the peace summoned a jury for this case. The verdict confirmed that Patrick Callaghan was guilty of the murder. He was then taken to Milford Jail. The Sheriff was accompanied by eight men armed with muskets and revolvers to transport the prisoner. They feared that the Irishmen would raid the wagon that the prisoner was in and free him. The Irishmen did attempt this, but the sheriff's men threatened to kill the first man who put his foot over the mark that they had made in the road. The Irishmen halted and turned back since they realized the guards were heavily armed.

Patrick Callaghan was imprisoned in Milford Jail. He was sentenced to be hanged, but Governor Johnson of Pennsylvania refused to sign his death warrant. The next Governor after Johnson was William Bigler. He also refused to sign the warrant. He said it was the responsibility of his predecessor to sign all death warrants of those convicted of murder during his term of office.

Due to this technicality, Callaghan was never hanged. He remained in Milford Jail for 5 years. When he was released, Callaghan went to Port Jervis to work as a brakeman on the Delaware Division of the Erie. He worked there for 20 years.

Twenty five years after the murder, he was run over by one of the train cars and died instantly. Ironically, this was only a few miles away from the spot where he killed George Kays.

Did the ghost of George Kays finally seek revenge on his killer? Could it be his ghost who haunts the jail where his killer was imprisoned? Or could it be the restless Lenni- Lenape Indians that Tom Quick had slaughtered many years ago? Maybe they have come back to regain their sacred land and become part of it for all eternity.

The Old Milford Jail
Milford, Pa. 2/2006
(Vortexes in front of me, after I was tripped)

JIM THORPE
2006

(THE OLD JAIL)

The Old Jail in Jim Thorpe, Pennsylvania was built in 1871. It was used as a county jail until 1995. This building was one of the finest 19th Century architectural jails ever built. It contains 72 rooms, including 28 cells, 16 dungeon cells and the original warden's apartment.

The Old Jail was in use until the 70's. It was named the Carbon County Jail. It is now a museum that is open to the public for ghost tours. The tour guide walks you through all the different areas in the jail. You can explore the main cellblock, the solitary confinement area in the basement, the gallows, and the famous Cell 17 that contains the mysterious handprint imbedded in the wall.

On June 21, 1877 seven men were hanged inside the main cellblock accused of being Molly Maguire's. Four men were hanged simultaneously facing each other. They had white bags over their heads. They could not look at each other. The trapdoors flung open and the bodies were left to hang there for 4 minutes before being cut down. The museum has the four nooses on display and a recreated platform where the men stood. It is pinpointed almost exactly to where the hanging took place. I was able to walk underneath this structure and stand on the floor where the bodies fell. I took a few pictures there. I felt a little eerie standing at this spot. So I took my photos and left abruptly. I felt a strong sense of sorrow in that particular area.

The Molly Maguire's were a secret organization, consisting mainly of Irish Catholics. They started one of the first labor movements in the country. The Irish were not well regarded by many facets of society at the time. There were very few jobs for these men. The only jobs they could get were working in the coal mines. The workers made only pennies for their long hours and horrible working conditions. This was considered slave labor. The men brought all their own work equipment from their bosses, and they also had to pay rent to them. The coal bosses owned their houses, and they could only shop at their employer's town store.

They felt this was an injustice. No wonder why they were found guilty of murdering coal management and vandalizing the mines and mining equipment. In 1875, Alec Campbell was hanged after being convicted of conspiracy in the murder of mine Superintendent John P Jones. On June 21, 1877, also known as "The Day of the Rope "or" Black Thursday", gallows were built to hang four persons simultaneously. The men were Alexander Campbell, John Donahue, Edward Kelly, and Michael Doyle. They were executed before a crowd of about 150 people in the main cellblock of the prison.

Before the hanging in 1877, one man, Alec Campbell, declared he was innocent. When Campbell was being ushered out of his cell on the way to the gallows, he is said to have resisted. He rubbed his hand in the dirt on the floor, and pressed his palm against the wall of the cell and proclaimed his innocence, stating "I am innocent." "There is no proof that I am guilty! But, this handprint on this wall will never go away and will be proof forever that they hanged an innocent man." It is still visible in cell 17 despite numerous attempts to remove it. The wall has been cleaned, and fresh concrete has been laid over it, but the handprint still continues to show up on the wall. Many scientists, archeologists, forensics experts, and paranormal investigators cannot find an explanation for this occurrence. In the 1930's, the local sheriff removed and replaced the plaster on the wall. A handprint formed at the same place on the new wall the day after it was completed. The handprint is the most unexplained phenomenon that has ever happened in Pennsylvania's Coal County. The hand print still remains there to this day.

From 1871 to 1995 there have been 3 suicides and one inmate's murder at the prison. This could be why there are spiritual energies trapped within the cellblock and dungeon.

Some of the phenomenon that has been reported is a shuffling sound in Cell 23, a creaking noise near the gallows, a blue light glowing in the solitary confinement "dungeon" and the soft sound of "booted footsteps." Also a woman's voice has been heard whispering.

The day I went on this tour, it was Memorial Day weekend, May 28, 2006. It was 100 degrees and very humid. I had to climb a bunch of cement stairs to get to the entrance. I was sweating profusely. The jail is built on a hill. The architecture of the jail is awesome. It is a brick building with high ceilings and huge wrought iron doors. It reminds me of a miniature medieval castle. When you enter the doorway you proceed to the right and sit down in a big waiting area. As you enter the jail there is a huge iron door. I couldn't even push the door open because it was so heavy. The guards must have been strong men to open and close these doors everyday. The architect who built this Jail also built the famous haunted jail "The Eastern State Penitentiary" in Philadelphia. This is the jail where Al Capone was an inmate. I had traveled to this jail also in April of 2006. It is also rumored to be haunted.

When I entered the main corridor, I didn't really feel anything until I passed by cell 17. This is where the famous handprint still exists today. I peeked in the cell and felt a little cold air escape from inside. It felt eerie. The cell is closed off and the door is locked so no- one can get close to the famous handprint. You are allowed to look only through the bars. The museum prohibits taking pictures of the phenomenon.

As my tour group was going downstairs, I lingered around the cell to snap a couple of pictures. When I tried to do this, my batteries in my camera were immediately drained and I was not able to take any photos. As soon as I walked away from the cell my camera seemed to work again. The indicator showed that the battery was fully charged. I proceeded downstairs to the solitary confinement cells to catch up with my group. I was able to take some pictures, but I didn't feel or see any activity. Luckily, my friend had a digital camera with her. She sneaked upstairs to get some pictures of cell 17. Just as she snapped a picture, her batteries started to drain.

After the tour was over, the guide said we could remain in the cellblock to look around. My friend's battery power was slowly recharging enough to take one last picture. Of course I ran over to Cell 17 and stood outside the cell while my friend snapped a quick picture of me. Then the camera died again. The batteries were completely drained. The picture came out a little blurry but if you look closely you can see there is some weird anomaly on the right side of my leg. It seems to be coming from inside the cell.

We finally left the jail and walked about 100 yards away. We both checked our cameras to see what type of batteries we were going to buy to replace them. We both couldn't believe what we were seeing. Both of the cameras batteries were restored and we were able to take pictures again. Suddenly it started raining heavily and the streets were flooding. The power went out in most of the restaurants and shops, so we decided to head back home. What an interesting way to end our spooky adventure.

Jim Thorpe Jail
Jim Thorpe, Pa. 5/2006
(I'm standing in front of Cell 17. Anomaly by my hip.)

HAWLEY
2005

THE SETTLERS INN

When I lived in Shohola, Pennsylvania, I traveled past the Settler's Inn numerous times. It is located in Hawley, Pennsylvania, which is about twenty five minutes from where I used to live. The Inn is a beautiful Tudor revival, across the street from Bingham Park.

From the outside, the building looks haunted. I was always intrigued with this Inn and I was curious to stop in and check it out. Since I am so fascinated with haunted houses, I decided to have dinner there for my birthday. Previously, I had read in a local ghost book that the Inn was haunted by a woman named "Hope". She died in the Inns' bakery, of a heart attack. The many strange occurrences that have happened here are usually associated with her spirit.

I asked our waitress if she experienced anything unusual while working at the Inn. She said, "Yes, the Inn is definitely haunted". "I remember one night I was cleaning up, getting ready for a party the next day". "I was folding napkins and arranging silverware on the table". "I was going about my business and I turned around for a second, and the silverware was moved, and the napkins and glasses were rearranged". She said at first she was frightened, but then she got used to this happening. She felt the spirit wasn't a threat and wouldn't harm her. It was a friendly ghost, and just a little bit of a nuisance. A couple of times, she had to yell at the ghost to stop moving the silverware. When she did this, it immediately stopped. She told me that only a few people have experienced this paranormal activity. The ghost is very docile, and for the most part very quiet. She only appears occasionally, usually downstairs.

Maybe this ghost remains anchored to earth because she was happy working here and she has some sort of emotional bond to this place. Perhaps she doesn't want to leave. She's just checking on things in the Inn, making sure everything is running smoothly.

One night on October 25, 2005, I drove past the Settlers Inn and I stopped to take some pictures. I took two photos. One was in front of the Inn and the other was on the right side of the building. The first photo didn't come out, but the second one did. It was taken on the side where there is a winding staircase, which is probably a fire escape. This side faces the street.

Once again, as in most of my photos, weird lines appeared when the film was developed. This photo, however, shows something a little different then the others, I have taken. It appears that ectoplasm is present in the left side of the picture.

Ectoplasm is residue that is left over by a spirit that was previously in a certain area. This residue leaves behind a peculiar appearance or physical disturbance in a haunted spot. Ectoplasm can take many forms. It can differ in color and intensity. It could look like a fog cloud, which sometimes a face or form can be seen within it. It could also be vaporous, look like plastic paste, or a membrane that oozes. This is the most common. The ectoplasm appears to look like a fine, fabric-like tissue. It can either be yellow, green, gray, or black. It is usually shows up white in photographs.

This substance usually helps ghosts materialize in some type of form. The residue is believed to be movement of spirits disturbing magnetic fields around the earth. Ectoplasm is also sometimes seen oozing around a psychic's body. This substance enables them to perform telekinetic power such as levitating tables, chairs, or other furniture. The ectoplasm forms into a spirit that possesses the body of a psychic. Usually the ectoplasm shows up better on film at night. You can see the white filmy substance a lot clearer. This is the reason I chose to take pictures in the evening.

The Settlers Inn
Hawley, Pa. 10/2005

SHOHOLA
2006

PEGASUS INN

Pat Edwards moved into the Pegasus Inn October of 1998. This Inn was owned by a couple of her friends John and Jose. She rented a room on the second floor. She told me a little bit about the history of the Inn.

At one time this was a summerhouse built in the early 1900's by a minister and his wife. There was a fire and everything was destroyed except the structure of the building. The house was rebuilt and has changed hands many times.

There were many gravestones found along the property surrounding the house. This may have indicated a burial ground. The history of these stones is unknown. Perhaps it was an ancient Indian burial ground? One of the owners, Jose was a college professor and he was very interested in ancient cultures. He was trying to research the stones to see how old they were. He contacted some archeologists. They were scheduled to come and check the gravestones, but they cancelled at the last minute. Unfortunately they had another appointment and were too busy to come and evaluate the tombstones.

Pat told me she thought the Inn was haunted when she first moved in. Eventually, by the time she moved out, she felt the spirits had moved on and left the Inn. She said she heard the most activity on the second and third floors. One night she could hear someone walking up the creaking stairs then proceed to walk down the hallway. It sounded like someone was opening and closing all the doors on the second floor. She peeked around the corner, but no one was there. On the third floor above her, she often heard someone walking around and slamming doors. It sounded like someone was walking up to the attic. These occurrences happened before the rooms were rented. She knew no one was occupying the two floors at this time. She was alone, except for the owners, who lived downstairs. Although the incidents were a little unsettling, she felt that the spirit was a non-threatening entity that just wanted to be noticed.

A few months later, a man named Joe, moved into a room on the second floor, which was down the hallway from Pat. I spoke to him about any weird occurrences that he might have experienced while living at the Inn. He said he also heard someone walking around upstairs. He also heard what sounded like several people talking in the empty rooms across from his. Sometimes the voices were so loud, it sounded like there was a party going on. The noise would wake him up. Then he would investigate the rooms and they would be eerily silent. There was no one to be found in any of the rooms.

There was a picture that hung in the hallway near his room. It was a black and white photo of the minister and his wife. It was taken in the early 1800's and looked very spooky. Joe swears that a few times he saw the eyes of the couple move back and forth when he walked past it. They seemed to be following his every move. He said he was so scared that he moved the picture downstairs to one of the sitting rooms.

I investigated the Inn on Thanksgiving 2006 and then again on Christmas Eve, 2006. The first time I recorded some EVPS on the second floor. I set up the digital voice recorder in the empty room across from Joe's room. When I played back the recording, I heard a very faint sound of movement in the room. It sounded like someone walking lightly on a creaking floor and then heavy breathing. This room was completely empty and there was no one on this floor at the time. On both occasions, orbs appeared in some of the photos outside as well as inside the house. The orbs appeared downstairs in the living room, not too far from the scary photo that Joe moved. The orbs outside appeared floating near the window of the empty room where Joe heard the voices and I recorded an EVP.

It seemed like there may have been several spirits in the house. During the fire in the early 1800's, some people died. No one knows for sure whom it was that perished in the flames. It could have been the minister and his wife or the mother of one of the owners. Pat says John's mother passed away in the downstairs bedroom of heart failure. John said that the only time he ever encountered anything unusual was a few days after his mother passed away in the house. He heard somebody rustling around in the kitchen and then walk into the bedroom where his mother stayed. That night he was brave enough to walk downstairs to see what was making the noise. He was startled by an apparition of his mother standing in the doorway of the bedroom. She smiled at him and looked very peaceful. He rubbed his eyes not believing what he was seeing. He was astonished to see her but he said he was not frightened. He felt like she came back one last time to say goodbye. He was very close to his mother and loved her dearly. This was the one and only time he ever saw her. Shortly after this incident, all paranormal activity ceased.

The Pegasus Inn
Shohola, Pa. 11/2006
(Orbs outside building.)

The Pegasus Inn
Shohola, Pa. 11/2006
(The Minister & his wife, their eyes move back and forth)
Early 1800's

MASSACHUSETTS

SALEM
2003-2007

WITCH HYSTERIA
1692-1697

In 1692, England and France were at war. Indians were attacking the ports and villages. Trade was impeded by the Pirates. A growing epidemic known as smallpox was infecting the villagers. The winter was very cold and long. Taxes were very high. At this time, many Puritans of New England believed the devil walked the earth. They also believed this bad fortune was the endeavors caused by the witches of Salem. They claimed the witches were the devil's practitioner's on earth causing these horrible events. This led to the witch trials of Salem. Many innocent women were accused of practicing witchcraft and were thrown into the dungeon or hanged. This increase of accusations and "witch hunting" became known as the witch hysteria.

The Puritans at the time believed the witch hysteria was due to poltergeist activity caused by an evil force. This contributed to the paranoia that the women experienced. Later this was discredited as a form of mass hysteria. One woman reacted a certain way, then several would follow the same pattern. It was like the power of suggestion. One person imposes an idea onto another and makes them believe it to be true, then that person tells others and it causes a chain-reaction of events.

The first incident of the witch trial began on January 20, 1692. Elizabeth Parris, 9 years old, and Abigail Williams, 11 years old, were the first girls to demonstrate strange behavior. They were experiencing blasphemous screaming, convulsive seizures, trance like states and mysterious fainting spells.

In February, physicians were unable to determine the cause of the symptoms. So they concluded the girls were under the influence of Satan and that they were witches.

Reverend Samuel Parris held prayer services and community fasting in hopes of relieving the evil forces that plagued Salem.

The girls were pressured to identifying what was causing the distressing events. They named three women that they claimed were witches. One was Tituba, their Carib Indian slave. On February 24, warrants were issued for the arrests of these women. Sarah Good and Sarah Osborne declared they were innocent. However, Tituba confessed to seeing the devil. She claimed he appeared to her as a hog or sometimes a great dog. She also testified that there was a coven of witches at work in Salem.

John Hathorne and Jonathan Corwin examined the three women in the meeting house in Salem Village. Tituba confessed to practicing witchcraft.

During the next few weeks, other townspeople came forward and testified that they, too, had been harmed by or had seen strange apparitions of some of the community members. Accusations were made against many different people.

Many women, whose behavior or economic circumstances were somehow disturbing to the social order and conventions of the time, were accused of witchcraft. Some women had previous records of criminal activity, including witchcraft, but others were faithful churchgoers and people of high standing in the community. One of them was Bridget Bishop, who was the wife of the governor.

One of the accused, Margaret Jacobs said, "They told me if I would not confess I should be put down into the dungeon and would be hanged, but if I would confess I should save my life."

The magistrates based their evaluations and judgments on various kinds of intangible evidence, including direct confessions, supernatural attributes (such as "witch marks" and reactions of the afflicted girls. There was also spectral evidence, which was based on the assumption that the devil could assume the "specter of an innocent person." This type of evidence was heavily relied upon despite its controversial nature.

The first person to be pronounced guilty of witchcraft was Bridget Bishop. This was the first official execution of the Salem Witch Trials. She claimed that she wasn't a witch and was innocent. However, she was condemned to death and was hung in Salem, Massachusetts.

Accusations of witchcraft escalated after her death. Many townspeople signed petitions on behalf of the accused people they believed to be innocent.

Among the many accused, were Rebecca Nurse, Susannah Martin, Sarah Wildes, Sarah Good and Elizabeth Howe. They were all executed. Others were taken to Gallows Hill to be hanged. These people were George Jacobs Sr., Martha Carrier, George Burroughs, John Proctor, and John Williard. Giles Corey was pressed to death for refusing a trial and pleading his innocence. The first person pleading innocent to confess was Dorcas Hoar. Her execution was delayed. In September, Martha Corey, Margaret Scott, Mary Easty, Alice Parker, Ann Pudeator, Wilmont Redd, Samuel Wardwell, and Mary Parker were hanged.

Thomas Brattle wrote a letter criticizing the witchcraft trials, after 20 people had been executed during the Salem Witch Hunt. After Governor Pheps read it, he ordered that reliance on spectral and intangible evidence no longer be allowed in trials.

The Superior Court was created by the General Court of the colony. They were in charge of the remaining witchcraft cases, which took place in May 1693. This time no one was convicted.

HOWARD STREET CEMETERY

I've been visiting Salem, Massachusetts every year for the past ten years. I've always been fascinated with the occult, ghosts, and witches since I was seven years old. Something always brings me back to this beautiful quaint little town on the harbor. Salem has about 40,000 residents. It has beautiful shops, hotels, and restaurants. It is located next to the Salem Harbor. At night however, this town can be very eerie and full of paranormal activity.

Salem and its ghost tours are initially what got me started on my quest for ghostly photographs. Year after year, I kept taking pictures of haunted areas but not capturing anything unusual on film. Finally, I decided to take some pictures at night. It was during October when the spirit world is the most active. When I developed the film, I finally got something. I was ecstatic. I had proof after all these years that there is something lurking in the shadows that most people cannot see but I certainly could sense.

I did some research and found out my pictures were vortexes, or moving orbs. This is believed to be energy of a spirit moving or trying to manifest itself. Since then, I have returned every year to the haunted spots of Salem and have gotten some sort of activity in almost every picture. One of the main areas is the Howard Street Cemetery.

This cemetery was opened in 1801. The last person buried there was in 1953. The grounds are where one of the most tragic and brutal murders in the name of justice was performed. This was the crushing of Giles Corey. Cory's wife was accused of witchcraft and imprisoned in a dark, dank dungeon. Giles pleaded with the Sheriff and the Magistrates. He wanted to be allowed to stay with his wife in the dungeon. They denied his request. Several weeks later, some teenage girls of Salem Village accused him of witchcraft. He was arrested shortly after.

Giles was asked how he would plea, but he remained quiet. He did not plea guilty or not guilty. Giles feared that if he spoke, by law, the Sheriff would confiscate all his goods and property. He also remained silent in contempt of the accusing girls, the Sheriff, and the Magistrate. Under English law, if a person did not plead one way or another, the punishment was a slow crushing under weights. This punishment was to continue until a plea was forthcoming or the person died. Those who pleaded guilty of witchcraft were reprieved but remained in jail, and those who pleaded not guilty were condemned to the guillotine.

Giles realized he would not get a fair trial and remained quiet. September 19, 1692, Giles was stripped naked and led to a pit in an open field. This field is now where the Howard Street Cemetery is located. Here he had to lie down in a pit. Six men placed heavy stones one by one on a door that was placed over his stomach and chest. They kept adding the stones on top of the door, slowly crushing him to death. He did not cry out in pain. His last dying words where "Damn you Sheriff! I curse you and Salem".

It seems every High Sheriff of Essex County since Corwin, suffered from Giles Cory's curse. All of the Sheriff's that were headquarted at the Salem Jail, which is located in the field where Giles was killed, died from a heart attack, or were forced to retire because of heart conditions or blood ailments.

Giley's ghost is said to appear before some impending doom is about to occur. He was last seen in 1914, when Salem suffered its greatest disaster. This was the Great-Fire that started at Gallows Hill. This is where 19 witches were hanged, including Giles's wife. She was killed three days after he was crushed to death. One third of the city was destroyed by the fire. Luckily, the houses in the historic districts were not harmed. They remained untouched from the flames.

I have an incredible photo of a face overlooking Howard Street Cemetery. It appears to be a man looking at the cemetery around the vicinity of where Giles was killed. Could this be him?

There are also swirling vortexes in the photo as well as an outline of what appears to be a horse in the sky. This is one of the most convincing paranormal photos I have taken. There seemed to be multiple spiritual manifestations occurring at the same time. It is fascinating.

The tour guide said there have been many people taking pictures of this particular area and they have gotten orbs and other various images that cannot be explained. Giles Corey's ghost has been seen numerous times, in the area that I photographed.

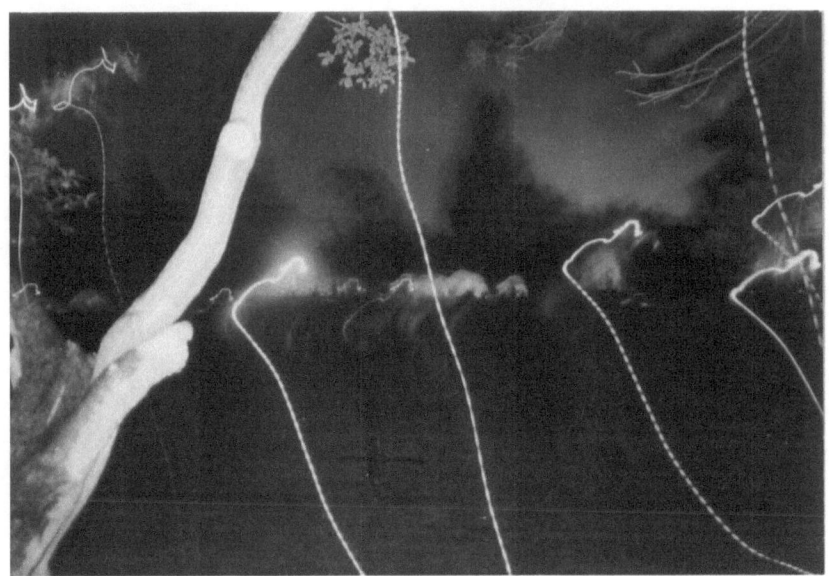

Howard Street Cemetery
Salem, Ma. 10/1998
(There is a face in the upper right hand side of the photo.)

Howard Street Cemetery
Salem, Ma. 10/19/98
(Location of where Giles Corey was pressed to death in 1692)

Howard Street Cemetery
Salem, Ma. 10/1998
(Vortexes coming out of the tombstones)

Howard Street Cemetery
Salem, Ma. 10/1998
(Vortexes in front of me, where Giles Corey was killed. This was Halloween
night; I was dressed as the Bride of Frankenstein.)

Howard Street Cemetery
Salem, Ma. 10/1998
(Vortexes protruding from the tombstones)

Howard Street Cemetery
Salem, Ma. 10/1998
(Field where Giles Corey was crushed to death)

OLD SALEM JAIL

The Old Salem Jail is located beside the Howard Street Cemetery. This jail was built in 1811. The jail became very over-crowded and closed in 1991 due to inhumane conditions. This is where the notorious Boston Strangler was imprisoned at one time. There were many murders, suicides, and hangings affiliated with this jail.

I've gotten pictures of numerous orbs surrounding the jail. No wonder there is so much spiritual activity roaming in this area. It's probably the lost souls of the prisoners who were bound to this horrible place so many years ago.

The Old Jail Keeper's House, also known as the Sheriff's Office, is also located in the vicinity of the Howard Street Cemetery and next to the jail. It was built in 1813 and destroyed by a fire in 1999.

The Sheriffs that worked there were the unfortunate ones that suffered from Giles Corey's curse. Every Sheriff that ever worked there died or suffered from some sort of heart ailment.

The Old Salem Jail
Salem, Ma. 10/1998
(Multiple vortexes and orbs in front of Jail)

The Old Salem Jail
Salem, Ma. 10/1998
(Intense multiple vortexes in front of Jail)

WITCH DUNGEON MUSEUM

The Witch Dungeon Museum has a live re-enactment of the witch trials and a tour of the re-created original dungeon. The original location of The Witch Dungeon is now the Federal building. This building was built over the dungeon. The museum however, has one of the original beams displayed downstairs that was retrieved from the original structure and moved to this location.

The museum was a church at one time and is reported to be haunted. There have been many sightings of a hooded man in a robe, resembling an ancient monk. He is usually seen near the "Crushing Scene of Giles Corey", and sometimes standing at a straw-roofed house that stands near the "Scene of the Gallows Hill Hanging." Many of the actresses working there have refused to escort tourists into the Dungeon in fear of seeing the hooded monk.

I took a picture outside the museum, and it looks like there are vortexes of spiritual activity in the crowd of people. The Federal Building at one time was the actual Witch Dungeon. It is located directly across from the Howard Street Cemetery. Here many innocent women died of starvation, and various diseases. These poor women suffered in tiny cells that were not even big enough to lie down. They had to constantly stand. They didn't have toilets or running water. Some stayed here waiting for their execution, while others remained there until they died.

The building has had many strange occurrences over the years. Many people that have worked there have left within a week, due to hearing voices, screams, moans, as well as seeing shadows and having objects thrown around. Several people from ghost tours have photographed numerous orbs floating around the building.

I took pictures in October 2005, during the time it was being renovated. There was alot of activity in the photos. I was very happy since previous years I was never able to catch anything. I went downstairs in this building to take photos. When I was there, I encountered strange phenomena. At one time, a small museum was located there. I was looking around taking photos. The woman working there told me weird things happen in the museum, everyday around the same time. This was from 3:00pm to 4:00pm. Just at that moment, I set a bottle of water down on the floor so I could read something. I glanced over at the bottle and noticed that the water inside was shaking. I looked at my watch and it was 3:15pm. It was really eerie because the room suddenly got cold and I felt like someone was staring at me. Perhaps there are still lonely spirits trapped here. Since this was the original Witch Dungeon, many innocent women died in the underground pits below. A lot of them starved to death and died of various diseases. It could be the spirits of the women who were accused of witchcraft haunting this place. They may be trying to get revenge for what happened to them.

The Witch Dungeon Museum
Salem, Ma. 10/2005
(Red vortexes outside the building)

The Witch Dungeon Museum
Salem, Ma. 10/2005

The original site of the Witch Dungeon Museum (Federal Building)
vortexes appear near the bottom floor.
Salem, Ma. 10/2005

JOSHUA WARD HOUSE

The Joshua Ward House is a beautiful colonial brick mansion located on Washington Street. It was built in the mid 18th century by a wealthy merchant named Joshua Ward. In 1789, George Washington slept on the second floor while on a visit to Salem, Massachusetts. For many years the building sat vacant and fell into disrepair. The Urban Renewal Project of Salem restored this building to its original majestic grandeur. This building was constructed on the foundation of a previous house formerly owned by the evil Sheriff George Corwin. In recent years, the building has been a realtor's office and a book binding company.

George Corwin was a cruel High Sheriff of Essex County. He tortured women who were accused of witchcraft and threw them in the Witch Dungeon. In 1692, he imprisoned 160 people, and confiscated all worldly goods of those executed at Gallows Hill. He put many innocent women to death. He was known as "The Strangler" because he used cruel methods of strangulation, to gain confessions. When George Corwin died in 1696, he was buried in the cellar of the Joshua Ward House. His family feared if he was buried in the cemetery, the angry people of Salem would dig him up and tear his body apart. After all, the townspeople hated him. Eventually many years later, his body was dug up and relocated to the Broad Street Cemetery.

His uncle was Jonathan Corwin, who was one of the judges in the infamous Witch Trials of 1692. He was responsible for hanging 19 witch's and having Giles Corey pressed to death. He resided at what is now is the historic Witch House on Essex Street. This is where the accused were often brought to be examined for supposed "Witch's marks".

The Joshua Ward House has a reputation of being very haunted. There have been many strange occurrences, mostly emanating from the third floor. This is where the majority of the hauntings take place.

In 1981, Richard Carlson bought this building and turned it into a real estate office. This is probably when the most paranormal activity has occurred. A few people have encountered a choking sensation upon entering a room on the second floor. Some have said they felt unseen hands grab them by the shoulders.

The most prominent ghost seen is a witch- like woman. An employee, who worked there, was taking Polaroid pictures of the staff to place on a Christmas Wreath. When the pictures were developed, one woman's photo didn't appear, instead was a picture of an old woman with white hair wearing a long gray coat. Need less to say, the woman was shocked and amazed at what she was looking at. It wasn't a reflection of herself but someone else. Another time, the same old woman was seen sitting in a chair in the waiting room. She resembled a mannequin. Her face seemed transparent, like you could see right through her. She had frizzled hair, and she seemed to be wearing an old Victorian dress from the 1800's. She was just sitting staring into space. When the customer glanced back at her, she noticed the old woman was gone. It was almost as if she vanished into thin air.

There have been many accounts of poltergeist activity throughout the building. Lampshades and waste baskets have been found turned upside down, books get thrown on the floor, and desk items are found scattered throughout the office when the employees return in the morning. The alarm has been set off 60 times in the past two years. The system has been checked several times and there is nothing wrong with it. Every time the police investigate they cannot find any signs of theft or evidence of a break in. One morning an employee found the brass candleholder upside down on the floor. One candle had melted in the shape of an s and the other in the form of a boomerang. According to the employees, the candles have never been lit. How can this logically be explained? It's possible the candles melted, but why would they take on that form? Someone would have had to shape the candles with their hands.

Down in the cellar where Corwin was buried, voices have been heard. Could there be more then one ghost haunting this house? Is the evil Judge Corwin still lingering here trying to torment and scare people even in death? Is he responsible for the choking sensation on the second floor? Is it his voice that has been heard in the cellar? Could the strange looking woman be Corwin's wife or one of the witches who were condemned to death by the hands of Corwin? Maybe she is haunting Corwin to seek revenge for her untimely and unjust death.

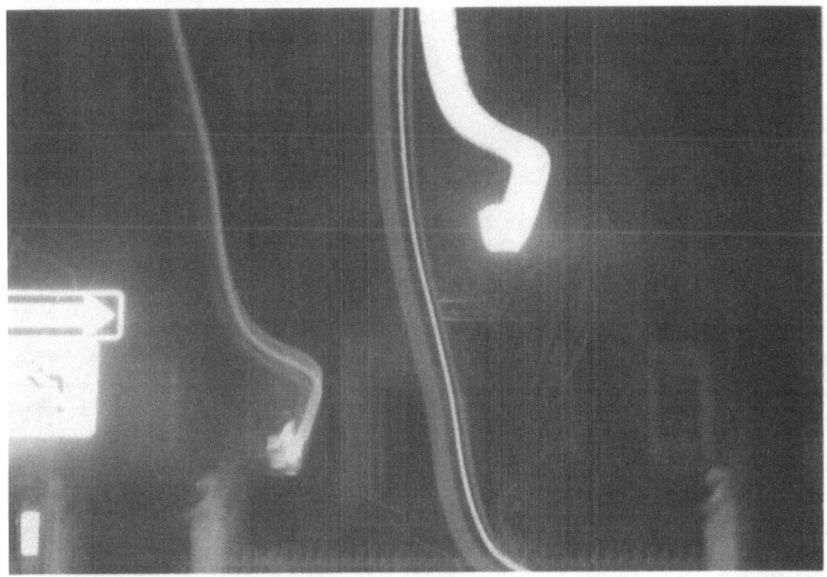

Joshua Ward House
Salem, Ma. 10/2003
(Vortexes appear from the upper floor)

Joshua Ward House
Salem, Ma. 10/2003
(Vortexes appear from the lower floor)

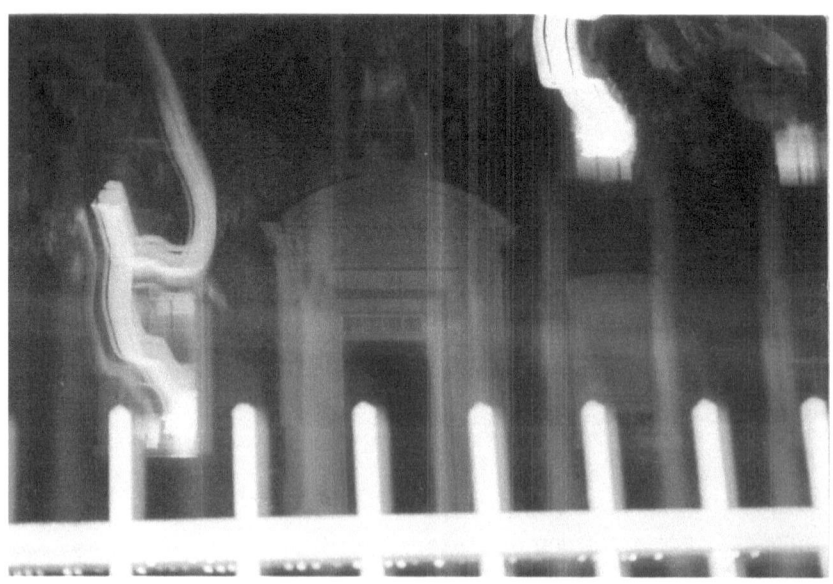

Joshua Ward House
Salem, Ma, 10/2003
(Vortexes appear from both floors)

OLD BURYING POINT

The Burying Point is the oldest cemetery in Salem. It is also known as the Charter Street Cemetery. It was established in 1637. It is the second oldest known cemetery in the nation.

There are many unique carvings and old interesting gravestones. This cemetery is located next to the Witch Trials Memorial on Charter Street. It contains many famous individuals such as Johnathan Corwin and John Hawthorne, who were judges in the Salem Witch Trials. Judge John Hawthorne was the great – great grandfather of writer Nathaniel Hawthorne. The judge had a very bad reputation. Nathaniel Hawthorne was so ashamed of his ancestor's role in the witch trials that he added a "w" into his last name to make it different.

The grounds of the cemetery are well kept and attempts have been made to restore most of the broken stones. At the entrance there is a plaque that contains information and a map which details where to find the most prominent citizens located in the cemetery. Samuel BroadStreet, who was governor of Massachusetts, and many more historical figures are buried here. There are a total of 347 entries for this cemetery.

In 1637, the town voted to set aside a point of land overlooking the South River as a burial ground. The site was probably already being used for that purpose. Many settlers who succumbed to the great sicknesses of 1628 and 1629 have been buried here. Among the prominent citizens the wife of Governor John Endicott is also buried here.

In 1637, John Home was given permission to erect and operate a windmill in the Burying Point, and John Cromwell was later granted the right to graze cattle there. The riverbank on the southern end of the Burying Point was filled with wharves and warehouses. In later years, additional land was acquired by the town for cemetery expansion. In 1767, the entrance was moved from Liberty Street to Charter Street.

When I went on the ghost tour for the first time here, I was enchanted by the huge old trees and the above ground tombs. There are many ancient looking gravestones that have been damaged by the acid rain. Some are so brittle they are crumbling into little pieces. Something summoned me to go to this cemetery. I walked through it several times during the night.

I took many photographs around Halloween at nighttime. Almost all of my pictures that were developed showed some type of paranormal activity. These are some of the most outstanding photos that I have in my collection. Many unexplained vortexes appeared that night. The Old Burying Point is what kept me coming back to Salem year after year.

Old Burying Point Cemetery
Salem, Ma. 10/2005
(Vortexes emanating from the tombstones)

Old Burying Point Cemetery
Salem, Ma. 10/2005
(Vortexes moving and forming into a shape of a tombstone)

Old Burying Point Cemetery
Salem, Ma. 10/2005
(Vortexes shooting straight up from the ground)

Old Burying Point Cemetery
Salem, Ma. 10/2005
(Swirling vortexes)

SALEM WITCH TRIALS MEMORIAL

In 1692, the Salem Witch Trials executions took place on June 10, July 19, Aug 19, Sept 19, and Sept 22. This memorial is dedicated to the 20 victims of the Salem Witch Hunt also know as the Witch Hysteria.

The Witch Trials Memorial was built in 1992 in honor of these victims. This tragedy happened over 300 years ago. The memorial is located next to the Old Burying Point, which is a historical cemetery. In October of 2005, I have photographed both these areas and have gotten evidence of spiritual activity in both locations. Over the years, I have taken many ghost tours that included this memorial and cemetery. The memorial is a very active and haunted place. I've captured on film many orbs and vortexes surrounding the entire area. The victims were actually not killed there. Many were hanged at Gallows Hill. Giles Corey was pressed to death in a field which is now the Howard Street Cemetery. I was at this memorial in October of 2005 around midnight when I took these extraordinary photos. There is always a higher level of activity in the month of October.

150 people were accused of witchcraft but only 31 were brought to trial in 1692. Six men were included. Nineteen were hanged, and 1 was pressed to death. Two women, Sarah Osborne and Ann Foster died in jail due to inhumane conditions. The women were starved, dehydrated and had to lay in their own urine and feces. They were shackled to the walls and had to sleep standing up. There was no medical treatment for them and many contracted diseases and died in the dark, dank cells.

Twenty people were victims of the Salem Witch Hunt. These names are engraved on the stones protruding from the walls surrounding the Witch Trials Memorial. This memorial is dedicated to these unfortunate souls.

The names of the victims were:

Bridget Bishop	George Burroughs	Martha Carrier
Martha Corey	Mary Easty	Sarah Good
Alice Parker	Mary Parker	John Proctor
Ann Pudeator	Wilmont Redd	Margaret Scott
Samuel Wardwell	Sarah Wildes	John Williard
Giles Corey	Elizabeth Howe	George Jacobs Sr.
Susannah Martin	Rebecca Nurse	

Salem Witch Trials Memorial
Salem, Ma. 10/2003
(Fast moving vortexes)

Salem Witch Trials Memorial
Salem, Ma. 10/2003

Salem Witch Trials Memorial
Salem, Ma. 10/2003

SAMUEL PICKMAN HOUSE

The Samuel Pickman house is located on 20 Liberty Street and the corner of Charter Street. It is next to the Witch Trials Memorial and the Old Burying Point.

The house may have been built in 1664, but the exact date of construction is unknown. It was owned by a mariner, named Samuel Pickman. Elizabeth Reardon, a Salem resident, originally discovered this 17th century dwelling under a Victorian mansard roof, and owned it for many years.

This is one of Salem's oldest buildings. It is considered to be a post Medieval or First Period building. The Historic Salem Inc. purchased this house in 1964, and partially restored it in 1969. The building needed major structural work, so it was sold to a private developer, who then completed the restoration. The Peabody

Essex museum purchased the house in 1983. It now has several offices there. I was unable to find any history on anyone who may have inhabited this house, or why it may be haunted. I have taken many photos of the Samuel Pickman House for four years in a row during October 2002- 2005. Halloween seems to be when the most activity appears. Colorful vortex's and orbs surrounding this house as well as streaks of light illuminating from the windows appear in these pictures. Since it's so close to the Witch Trials Memorial, the spiritual activity may be attributed to the wandering spirits of the innocent women who were hanged there.

Samuel Pickman House
Salem, Ma. 10/2003
(Vortex appears shooting out of the windows)

THE HOUSE OF THE SEVEN GABLES

Listed on the National Historic Register of Historic Places is the House of Seven Gables. This house is now a museum which includes a guided tour. It is located at 54 Turner Street in Salem, Massachusetts. It sits over looking the Salem Harbor.

It has an 18th Century granite sea wall, and two seaside Colonial Revival Gardens. Inside the house, there are more then 2000 artifacts and objects, consisting of over 40 framed pictures, 500 photographs, numerous glass plate negatives, more then 650 books in the library and a mysterious secret staircase.

This house was built in 1668, and is the oldest surviving 17th Century wooden mansion in New England. It is also know as the Turner-Ingersoll Mansion. It was named after the two families that lived there. The Ingersoll family purchased it after one of the Turner sons lost the family fortune.

Nathaniel Hawthorne's cousin, Susan Ingersoll, lived in the house until she was 72 years old. Nathaniel visited her often. This house inspired him to write the novel, "The House of the Seven Gables". Many years later, the house where Hawthorne was born, was moved just feet away from this mysterious mansion. It is now a museum that is also open to the public.

In 1908, Caroline Emmerton, and architect Joseph Everett Chandler restored its original seven gables. Her goal was to pre-serve the house for future generations, and to provide educational opportunities for visitors. She used the proceeds from the tours to fund her settlement programs.

This mansion has a reputation of being haunted. Several people have claimed to have seen the ghost of Susan Ingersoll roaming the hallways and peering out the windows. There have been rumors that Nathaniel Hawthorne's son haunts the attic area. He has been heard playing with his toys and roaming around the attic. Many visitors and employees have heard toilets flush on their own, and the faucets turn on and off by themselves.

When I was browsing the internet doing some research on this house, I came across a website of ghostly photographs. There is a picture of a small boy looking over a fence near the garden. Could this be Hawthorne's son, who died very young, or could there be some negative energy surrounding the house because Nathaniel Hawthorne was a descendent of a witchcraft judge.

I took a picture right before sunset, while I was waiting for the tour to begin. I felt something strange in the air and turned around to take one last photo of this beautiful mansion. Of course with my naked eye all I could see was the house and garden. However, when this film was developed, I was looking at one of my best photos ever taken. It was a picture of numerous colorful vortexes intertwining with each other producing an eerie photo of spiritual activity. It almost looks like a very colorful sunset.

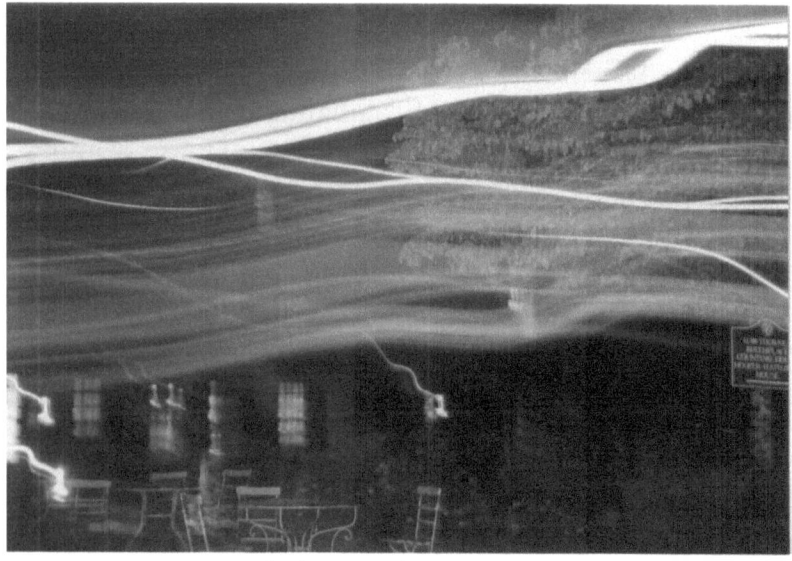

The House of Seven Gables
Salem, Ma. 10/2005
(Intense colorful vortexes)

PHANTOM SHIPS

In 1630, the Puritans settled Salem, Massachusetts. They reported seeing a "specter ship" that sailed backwards. It looked like there was one man and one woman on the deck. They were presumed to be lovers sailing the seas for eternity, in reverse. This ship seems to appear and disappear suddenly.

This is just one of the many phantom ships seen on the New England coastline.

Another haunted ship is the Grampus, which was named at one time the "CAN DO". The Global Hope is a 628- foot oil tanker. It was anchored off Coney Island Ledge in Salem Sound, carrying 2.1 million gallons of oil. During the Great Blizzard of 78, The Global Hope smashed into Coney Island Ledge. The hull broke and the engine room flooded. The blizzard produced 60-mile an hour winds and 20-foot seas with zero visibility.

The owner of the "CAN DO" decided to head out of Gloucester Harbor to rescue the GLOBAL HOPE.

A giant wave hit the ship and smashed the windshield and sliced the owner's arm. The "CAN DO" was three miles off Salem Harbor. The radar was down and the crew died. Two bodies were found off Nahant, and two more were found on Marblehead beach. The ship was found underwater off Tinkers Island, Marblehead. A body was found in the engine room.

The ship was towed into Salem's North River to be repaired. The hull and cabin were severely damaged.

In January 1983, the present owner of the CAN DO, was welding in the engine room one night when he heard voices coming from down below at the bow. He went to look, but no one was there. He was all alone.

On October 31, 2005, I went to Salem Harbor on a haunted cruise ride during "Haunted Happenings". This is a month long celebration for Halloween. It includes various activities like parades, trolley rides, haunted houses, and storytellers throughout the city of Salem. This city is the Halloween capital of the world. There are street vendors, and some roads get shut down due to the huge amounts of tourists roaming the streets. Many people get dressed up; it's similar to Mardi Gras in New Orleans.

This particular Halloween, it was very cold and windy. The cruise took us out about 20 minutes into open water, and 20 minutes back. The storyteller told us many tales about phantom ships, pirates, and people drowning all along the coastline of the Salem Harbor. It was hard to believe that these horrible things actually happened. I took a few pictures along the shoreline. I was amazed to see activity in these pictures when they were developed. I just aimed my camera at the shoreline and shot photos into the darkness, not expecting to see anything out of the ordinary. In the pictures, I saw numerous strands of lights illuminating from the water. It seemed like all the ghosts were hanging out near the harbor. They were probably trying to get away from all the chaos going on in the streets of Salem on Halloween night. Could this energy be from all the sailors who crashed on the shoreline and perished?

Salem Harbor
Salem, Ma. 10/2003
(Picture taken from the boat in complete darkness.
No light source from the shoreline)

STOCKBRIDGE
1993

THE RED LION INN

I had a recurring dream for years throughout my childhood and into my mid-twenties. In the dream, I was a servant wench working in a tavern serving food and spirits. The bar was down-stairs and the lodging was upstairs. I can remember the hallways were so dark and dreary that I had to light a candle so that I could see the rooms. This tavern was very old; it probably dates back to the 1800's. The rooms and hallways were furnished with Victorian furniture and paintings.

In my dream, I am walking upstairs headed towards one of the rooms. When I arrive, I open a door and I feel a strong wind pulling me into a vortex in the middle of the room. I can sense an overwhelming evil presence engulfing me. My chest feels tight and it is hard to breathe. Something is keeping me from leaving the room. I look over to the right and I see a closet door. When I open the door, I see a crack in the wall. The wind starts blowing violently and I am suddenly surrounded by white doors with shutters on them. I try to open them but they are all locked. I am trapped inside the closet and I cannot get out. I then hear someone whis-pering my name. The voice gets louder and louder. I turn around trying to decide which is the right door to open. I have an over-whelming desire to get outside this closet. I'm starting to panic now because I can't find my way out. Then I feel a hand grab mine and pull me outside into the hallway.

As soon as I am out of the closet, I feel automatically better. I can breathe again and it feels like a weight has been lifted off my chest. I am finally away from the evil presence. Then I run through the hallway downstairs to the tavern. The dream suddenly ends.

When I was in my mid-twenties, a former boyfriend and I decided to get away for the weekend. He would not tell me where we were going because he wanted it to be a surprise. I was not sure where he was taking me. I only knew it was a place in Stockbridge, Massachusetts. We arrived that night at the Red Lion Inn, one of the most historic Inns in the United States.

I remember how amazed I felt at being there and how beautiful the place was. It seemed familiar to me. Was I experiencing deja vu'? It was almost like I was here before. When I walked inside, I noticed the rooms were filled with 17th and 18th century furniture. There was a bar downstairs, and the rooms upstairs, just like in my dream. Also, when we got to our room, there was a bed to the right, a painting above it, and a closet all on the same side. It was almost identical to the haunted room in my dream. However, there were no cracks on the wall inside the closet. I felt a little relief. I was hoping I wouldn't have a reoccurrence of my dream.

The only strange thing that occurred that night was when I was getting ready to take a shower. I turned on the faucet and boiling hot water burned only my wrists and ankles. The water went directly to these areas with such precision, it was bizarre. Then I suddenly had a flashback that I was a witch bound by chains around my wrists and ankles and I was being burned alive. It was pretty scary. I thought to myself, maybe I was reincarnated. Could this be why I remember this place so vividly? Is it possible that I lived here, or worked here back in the 1800's? Somehow I felt connected to this place, but I wasn't sure why.

When I was doing some research on the history of the Red Lion Inn, I discovered there was a fire in 1896. The original structure was destroyed. The Inn was restored and rebuilt over the years. In the early 19th century artists and intellectuals discovered this area. It became a famous summer retreat.

Illustrator Norman Rockwell maintained a studio across the street from the Inn. His famous "Main Street, Stockbridge", was inspired by the Inn. This was during the 1950's Christmas season.

If I was reincarnated, did I live in Massachusetts ? Could this be why I am so intrigued with Salem ? Could I have been one of the witch's who were burned alive at the stake during the Witch Hysteria of 1692? I'm not sure if I believe in reincarnation or not. Reincarnation is the belief that when you die, your soul leaves your body and is reborn into another body. So every time there is a death at that moment there is a birth. And sometimes you may remember bits or pieces of your previous life. Could this be what I experienced? Could my dream be actually a memory of long ago? I can only remember my past in a dreamlike state. This is perhaps why people are hypnotized; it helps them recall better being in a semi- conscious state rather then when they are awake.

I'm not sure if this is an explanation to the incident that happened to me, but it is uncanny that I keep returning to Massachusetts every year, as if something is beckoning me.

PLYMOUTH
2006

BURIAL HILL

This ghost tour was one of the most labor intensive and physically challenging walking tours I have ever taken. We had to climb 50 steep concrete steps in order to arrive at the first location on the ghost tour. On this hill is a statue of an Indian chief in a full headdress. This is where a huge sarcophagus was placed to bury the Plymouth residents as well as the Indians.

According to the news, it had been raining all week in Plymouth. The night we arrived it had finally stopped raining and the sky cleared up. It was a nice night for a ghost tour. It was May 6, 2005. The tour consisted of my friend and I and only three other people. It was very informative and the guide was able to tell us additional stories since it was such a small group. We had to do a lot of walking and then we had to climb another set of steps to get to Burial Hill. The cemetery is literally on top of a hill overlooking Plymouth, Massachusetts. I have never been in a cemetery that had such a high elevation. Burial Hill has enormous trees spread throughout the cemetery and is very well maintained. It is very beautiful and peaceful but there is a slight eerie feeling at night.

During the tour, one of the guides was trying to get an EVP recording (Electronic Voice Phenomenon) in a different section of the cemetery. I was taking pictures of haunted hot spots of activity. I was able to capture vortexes surrounding some of the tombstones. Burial Hill was the site of the first fort. It was a meeting house and place of worship before it became a cemetery. It dates back to colonial times. It is the oldest cemetery in Plymouth, Massachusetts.

The engravings on the older tombstones have a lot of symbolic meaning to them. Almost every mark on the tombstone represents something significant to the deceased.

The most common engravings are the "skull" or "dead head". The skull is usually seen with wings or crossbones. In the 1800's, people wanted to get to heaven when they die. They believed if they had wings or angels engraved on the headstones it would enable them to fly to heaven when they died. The different images in the tombstones are called effigies.

There are also different types of tombstones. The single tympanum is the most commonly seen. It has a single arch at the top of the stone. The second stone is called the double tympanum; it has two arches at the top. This stone is not as frequently seen in cemeteries. Plymouth residents bought their slate from England, which was very expensive. It would be a very costly procedure to obtain this type of tombstone. Older tombstones were made of one of the three different types of stone.

These are blue slate, brimstone, and purple slate. The blue slate is actually bluish- gray in color and is the most common tomb-stone in the 16 & 1700's. This was cheaper then purple slate but stronger then brimstone. The brimstone tombstones are bleached white. This type of tombstone is not often seen. The purple tomb-stones are actually a purple -red color. This type of tombstone is the most expensive and seen the least out of the three. Only people of royalty or wealth could afford these headstones.

Since the 1620's, Plymouth residents used the hill as a burial site. The first English settlers were the Pilgrims. They built their first fort and meeting house here.

The Mayflower passengers are buried in this cemetery. Governor William Bradford and William & Mary Brewster are also buried here. The last burial in this cemetery was in 1957. The earliest grave markers were carved of wood, and did not survive the harsh weather. In the mid seventeenth century stone markers were used. The oldest know stone in Burial Hill is that of Edward Gray. It dates back to 1681. These early stone markers are valuable historic documents, and many are irreplaceable works of folk art.

The Pilgrims built a sarcophagus to bury their dead. Indians were also buried within the sarcophagus. The Native American Indians were buried in a fetal position. Inside the sarcophagus the left side was for the women and the right side was for the men. The Indian bones were buried with their artifacts. The women were buried with pottery, cooking utensils, etc. The men were buried with hunting tools such as bows, arrows, knives and hatchets. The Pilgrims on the other hand, were buried in a straight fashion with nothing of value alongside their bodies. There were no grave-stones for the bodies, so it was impossible to distinguish whom the people were and whether they were male or female.

In the 1800's and 1900's, grave robbing was very popular among medical students. There were many underground medical schools. The only way you could become a student at these schools was to bring your own cadaver for dissection. Once the students learned how to dissect the human body they would be considered a doctor. In order to complete this gruesome act, many students would get their own picks and axes and dig up tombs in Plymouth and steal dead bodies. Another haunted area we walked to was called the Village Square. This area contained the pillars, church, and courthouse. Ships from Boston would sail into Plymouth harbors and ports.

One stormy December the ship could not make it into port. It got stuck in a sandbar due to a low tide. The Plymouth residents found the ship the following morning and boarded the deck. They witnessed a gruesome sight. All the men were frozen to death. They carried the bodies to the town brook to thaw them out. Then they were transported to the biggest building, which was the courthouse, to store the bodies until they were buried. These unfortunate sailors haunt the courthouse. Sometimes faces of these men can be seen in the bottom windows.

In the Village Square there is a church. This is where the pillar stocks were located. The accused criminals that were on their way to the stocks would hang their faces down in shame. The townspeople were very cruel and threw rocks and trash at them. The town officials hammered long nails through their ears into the back of the wood to keep their heads facing upward. This was painful and humiliating. When it was time for them to come down from the pillars, they would take a knife and cut the nail out of the ear. Pieces of flesh from the ear would still remain on the pillars. This was done to create fear in the town. It also was a way to haunt the accused criminals for the rest of their lives reminding them of the crimes that they committed.

The gallows were another form of punishment. They were located at Merdock Hill, which was behind Burial Hill. One of the barbaric methods of punishment was to force a person to climb up a ladder that was resting against the gallows and put a noose around their neck and then jump off the ladder enabling them to hang themselves. Of course, some people were reluctant to taking these orders. So they were pushed off instead. Their bodies would be suspended in the air shaking violently. The townspeople believed that was the evil spirits coming out of the person's body. The superstition was that if you walked under the ladder that was against the gallows you would get possessed and take on the characteristics of that person.

Our tour guide said on a previous tour there was a group of about 25 people. They all had an eerie encounter in Burial Hill Cemetery. When they entered the cemetery all of their cameras stopped working. Everyone got cold and their hair started to stand up on end. It was the middle of August and the temperature was still in the 90's. There was no explanation for the sudden change in temperature. One of the tour guides measured it to drop down to 40 degrees. Several people who had flashlights noticed that their batteries had been drained. Someone saw a tall dark figure standing near a tree. He decided to film it with his camcorder, but the batteries suddenly died. He couldn't understand this because he had just put in new batteries before entering the cemetery.

It has been a theory that ghosts tend to drain the energy from the atmosphere as well as from cameras, batteries and flashlights in order for them to manifest.

During the tour, a guide picked up fluctuations in temperatures as he walked past the area where the shadow was seen. Also a woman said she sensed an eerie feeling standing near a tombstone. She claimed to have felt someone standing behind her blowing on her neck. Could this be the ghost of Anna who is rumored to walk this cemetery at night? After all, she was standing right next to her gravestone. This is the most active area of the cemetery.

Vortex in Burial Hill Cemetery
Plymouth, Ma. 5/2006

NEW JERSEY

CAPE MAY
2005

THE SALTWOOD INN

The Winward House is a beautiful Edwardian seaside home. In 1905, George Baum built this house for his wife and family. He was a wealthy businessman from Philadelphia.

The Saltwood Inn was rumored to be built for his mistress, Catherine. This B & B was built next door to the Windward House. There are heart-shaped cutouts on the shutters and interior railing of both houses. This was supposedly designed for his lover.

The ghost of Catherine is believed to walk between the two houses. The Winward House was refurbished in 1972. It was an old private residence at the time. This was one of the first new B& BS that replaced Cape May's perennial boarding houses.

There have been reports from several people staying at the B&B that they have sensed a feminine presence on the third floor. Another person witnessed a woman wearing a shimmering gold fabric dress. Guests have also seen a mysterious woman cleaning the room. Footsteps moving back and forth and banging noises have been heard on the third floor deck, late at night when no-one is around.

It is also rumored that perhaps the ghost is an Irish servant named Bridget. She has been seen in the "Wicker Room" on the third floor.

On the second floor, the owner experienced something go right through him. Also, the ghost of a middle-aged woman was seen going up the steps.

The Saltwood Inn was built between 1905 and 1906 after the Winward House. The owner claims there has been ghostly activity on the third floor. He thinks it may be a ghost of a former servant. A friend of the owner experienced the ghost of a woman at the foot of her bed. The ghost gave her name, she said it was Catherine.

A psychic claimed that he could contact a female spirit that told him she once lived next store. She claimed to be the lover of the man who once lived in the Winward House. When the man passed away Catherine continued to mourn him. She said that after the man's wife died, the house was sold. The spirit told the psychic that when she was alive she had intended to buy The Winward Inn but she passed away before this could happen. Therefore, she started haunting the house.

In the 1800s, James and Catherine Mooney owned much of the property on the side of Jackson Street. Catherine outlived her husband. Since his wife's and lovers name were both Catherine, it is not certain who actually haunts this B & B. Could it be his wife who was attached to the home and refused to leave? Or George's mistress who is endlessly roaming the halls at night mourning her lover?

There have been screams heard at the Inn, and footsteps in the middle of the night pacing back and forth in the Wicker Room.

One thing is for sure, the Saltwood Inn is still very active to this day. What a beautiful place the ghost chose to haunt.

Saltwood Inn
Cape May, NJ. 7/2004
(Strange L-shaped vortexes appear on the 3rd floor)

MAINE

YORK
2005

OLD GOAL JAIL

This picture was taken on the ghost tour in York, Maine on September 2, 2005. It is in front of the Old Goal Jail. This may be the ghost of Patience Boston, who was imprisoned there. Patience was a wild Indian woman who was accused of killing the local minister's son.

The townspeople accused her of drowning him in the well. She said the allegations were not true and she was innocent. She claimed that the boy was a trouble maker and he was always underfoot. The suspicion was that he most likely fell into the well and died accidentally. There wasn't any sufficient proof that she committed this crime or had anything to do with his unfortunate death. There were rumors that she had an affair with the town Judge. He locked her in jail to keep her quiet. He was afraid that she may expose their scandalous affair, so he blamed her for killing the child.

However, she was sentenced to two years in the Old Goal Jail. She was pregnant at the time, so she only remained here until she gave birth to her child. Immediately, her baby was taken away from her. Three days later, she was hung on the property.

Some people believe she still haunts the upstairs room, where she was once held prisoner. Her ghost has also been known to roam the streets and nearby cemetery.

Legend says, if you listen closely outside the front of the jail, you may hear the sounds of a woman weeping. Perhaps, she is still looking for her baby that was taken away from her so many years ago.

When I was on the ghost tour, I felt like someone was standing behind me. Everyone was focused on the jail and the tour guide. They were looking straight ahead at the building. I kept looking over my shoulder to see if something was behind me.

When I turned around, I noticed this huge bush next to the property that the jail was on. Instead of taking a picture of the jail, I decided to take a picture of this bush. I felt like a strong presence was there.

It was a clear, warm, night, so there was no explanation for why the photo came out this way. I was shocked when I developed the picture. There were prominent white vortexes interlocking with each other. It looks so intense. Maybe the lines express the emotions of this woman!

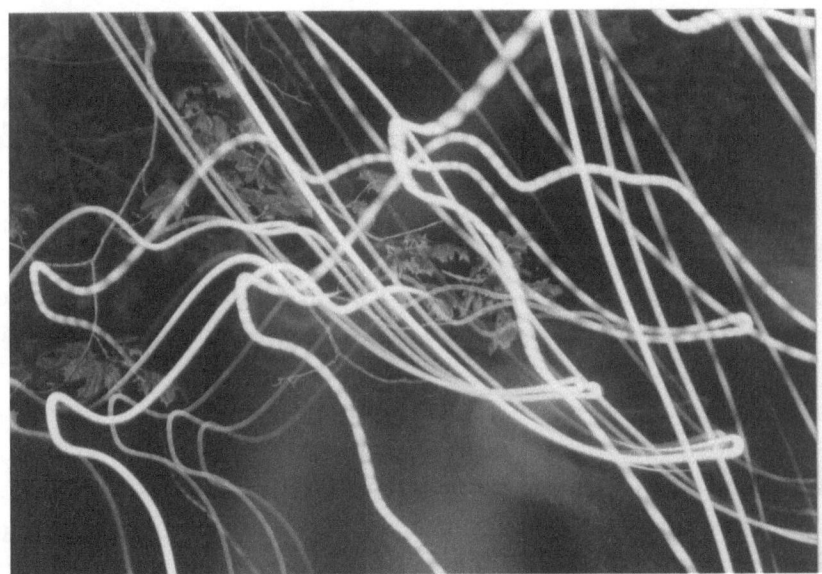

The bush near the Old Goal Jail
York, Maine 9/2005

THE LADY OF YORK, MAINE

Across the street from the Old Goal Jail is a house that is reported by many village residents as being haunted. This is a two story Victorian house. On the upper floor, a lady in a long black dress has been seen through the window. She appears to be walking back and forth, sometimes looking out the window. It's almost as if she is waiting for someone.

Some residents of the village of York have noticed her at all different hours of the night. This house has been vacant for years. One person spotted this woman and called the police so that the house could be inspected for illegal trespassing. No one was found on the premises or in the abandoned house. At one time, the windows were boarded up to discourage any vandals from getting inside the house. There were many phone calls to the police regarding a strange woman wandering around inside. The police could never find any evidence that anyone was there.

During the time the windows were boarded up there weren't any sightings of this woman. All ghostly activity ceased.

When the house was put up for sale, the boards on the windows were removed and the ghostly woman re-appeared once again, walking around the house. No one knew who this woman could be. Maybe she lived in this house many years ago and her energy still remains.

I took a photo of this house on September 2, 2005. A thick green line, or vortex, appeared near the top floor where the ghost of the woman has been seen.

This could be evidence of a residual haunting. This is when the ghost performs the same sequence of events over and over again. It is similar to a tape being recorded and played back several times.

The law of physics states that energy cannot be created or destroyed. Our bodies are made up of energy. So when we die, where does the energy go? I like to believe we all move on to another plane or dimension. For those who don't move on, either they're stuck or perhaps they don't want to leave this plane due to unfinished business. Perhaps there is a residual energy left over inside this house from the previous owner. Her energy could have been recorded or stored in the nails of the house or any old furniture she was attached to. Perhaps, she is feeding off areas of the house that required lots of physical excursion, such as steps. She would need this residual energy in order to manifest herself repeatedly.

STATUE OF CONFEDERATE SOLDIER

This is another picture that was taken on the ghost tour in York, Maine on September 2, 2005. This statue is in the center of York Village. It is very unusual because it is a statue of a Confederate soldier. Since Maine is a northern state, the statue most likely should be a Union soldier. It is strange that the residents of the town would erect this monument since it was the South that they were fighting against.

This statue doesn't have much history, but it's been know to weep during certain times of the year. Several people have witnessed the statue crying real tears.

Something was drawing me to this statue of a Confederate soldier during the walking tour. I couldn't concentrate on the tour guide. I just kept looking at the statue. I thought, after the tour was over, I would go back to it and take a picture. It was very hard to get to because it is located at a very busy intersection. Cars were speeding around it, and it was very difficult to cross the street to get to the statue. However, I was very persistent and determined to take this picture. I finally made it across the street and got close enough. I zoomed in with the camera, trying to focus on the statue's face. I was hoping I might get a picture of the soldier crying.

Instead, when I developed the film, I was very excited and surprised to see that there was fog-like mist and white lines surrounding the statue. It was weird because it was a clear night. There wasn't any rain, fog, or wind to interfere with the picture. The weather was perfect. It was amazing that this picture captured all these elements. I'm glad I followed my intuition and didn't give up trying to get this photo. According to this picture, it seems there is a spirit trapped inside this statue. Could it be the spirit of someone who was killed in war? Or is there something else that haunts this statue?

The fog surrounding this statue is possibly ecto-mist. It is a form of ectoplasm. When caught on film, it appears to look like fog or shadows. Typically, ectoplasm is seen in the form of an oozing substance that is yellow, green, or white. It usually has been known to appear oozing from the mouth and nostrils of a psychic during a séance. This is said to occur because the spirit is trying to manifest itself, by using the psychic as a conductor. Sometimes, it can appear in a ghost-like form. This substance usually is affiliated with a spirit trying to take human form. They draw off this whitish substance.

The conditions have to be right in order for ectoplasm to appear. Not only was the weather perfect that night, but there was also a lot of energy in the air. Also, the spirit has to be willing to show itself.

This night, I believe, it wanted to appear to me. This is why I got such an extraordinary picture.

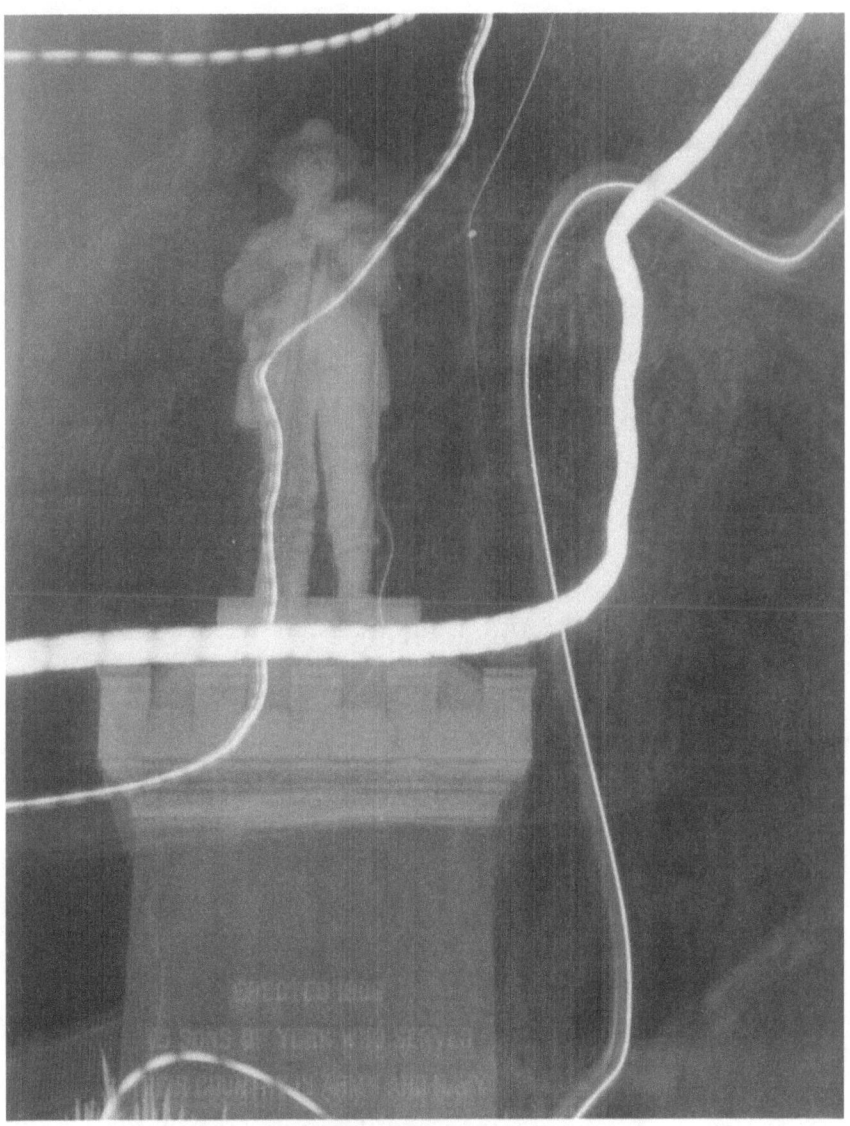

Statue of a Confederate Soldier
York, Maine 9/2005
(Vortexes and ecto-mist surrounding the photo)

NEW YORK

NEW YORK CITY
2004

OLD MERCHANTS HOUSE MUSEUM

The Old Merchant's House was built in 1832. It is a Greek revival brick townhouse. This building is located between Greenwich Village and the East village in Manhattan, NYC. It is the only early 19th Century New York building that has its original exterior, interior, and furnishings.

The "old merchant" was Seabury Treadwell. He purchased this building three years after it was built. Treadwell was a partner in a marine hardware supply firm. He had a wife and six daughters. Three of the girls never married and died at home. Mr. Treadwell was very strict and felt many of the male suitors were not good enough for his daughters. He scrutinized every man who tried to date his daughters.

One of his daughters, Gertrude, lived here her entire life until she died in 1933. She is believed to haunt this house. Many people have seen her ghostly form.

Her father was very protective and domineering. He didn't allow her to marry the great love of her life. This drove her into a life of seclusion. After her father died in 1865, Gertrude and her sister Phoebe lived together in the big house. They waited until sunset before they went outside, to avoid as many people as possible.

Gertrude died in 1933. Three years after Gertrude passed away, the house was turned into a private historic site and museum. It is listed on the National Register of Historic Places and it is open for public tours by a private foundation. Some architectural surveyors and researchers experienced some strange occurrences while they worked there. They have heard the piano playing in the parlor although there was no one there.

Some other weird occurrences that happened were misplaced items mysteriously showing up after they had been lost, laughing and sighing sounds coming from the tea room, and a aroma of fresh flowers when there were no-one in the rooms.

In the 1930's, a woman was cataloging Gertrude's wardrobe. She claimed to have seen an apparition of a woman dressed in Victorian clothing descend down the staircase. This ghostly woman has also been seen near the fireplace in the kitchen and several other locations throughout the house.

A psychic claims there is a high intensity of energy in the house. He sensed most of the spirit activity is concentrated near the upstairs fireplace. He also felt that it was feminine, sad, and alone.

A former volunteer said that she sat at a table in the kitchen and a strange force guided her to involuntarily write- not in her own handwriting but in a classic style of longhand. This is known as automatic writing. She wrote the words: Miss Treadwell is here.

I have photographed this building three times in hopes of getting something paranormal in the picture. The first two times I didn't get anything. The third time I finally did. I was so happy that I didn't give up because I had a gut feeling I would capture something in the photo. I could feel the energy surrounding the building and it felt very active that night. I took two photos in front of the building. They were only seconds apart. In the first photo, everything appears to be normal. In the second, you can see an apparition of a woman's face floating in the air close to the second floor. It looks like she is wearing a Victorian, white hat and dress. She has dark black hair. Her appearance matches the description of Gertrude Treadwell.

I was amazed at the clarity of this photo when it was developed. The only other picture that I have of an apparition is from Howard Street Cemetery in Salem, Massachusetts. This is one of the first ghost photos that I have taken that have shown paranormal evidence. This photo in particular is so extraordinary because it is very hard to catch a full body apparition on film. It is very rare and a ghost hunters dream to capture such evidence.

I am so glad that I didn't give up and kept pursuing photographing this building. It was well worth the several trips to New York City in order to achieve this.

My interest was peeked by seeing this. Shortly afterwards I started going on numerous ghost tours. I wanted to take pictures of as many haunted places as possible.

Old Merchants House
Greenwich Village, NYC 4/2004
(A woman's face is floating in the air on the right side of the photo.)

VIRGINIA

RICHMOND
2006

GOVERNORS MANSION

Richmond is Virginia's state capital. It is a regional center for business and education with nine Fortune 500 companies based in the city. There are many prestigious schools such as Virginia Commonwealth University and the University of Richmond. There are many historic mansions and beautiful old parks. Richmond has many Civil War sites and monuments.

There is a section of Richmond called Carytown. This is where I like to go every time I visit. There are many trendy little shops and unique restaurants located here.

Another popular part of town is called Shockoe Bottom. There are many night clubs and bars. This is where the Haunted Richmond Tour headquarters is located.

In addition to the tour, for a small fee, you can experience a live show with re-enactors. Several of the local haunted legends & locations that are on the tour are featured here. It is very good and I highly recommend it.

My friend and I went to Richmond, Virginia to visit her aunt and mother. I was so excited when I found out that there was a ghost tour in the down town area. This was the most physically challenging ghost tour that I have ever been on. It was around 8:00pm but it was still about 100 degrees outside. The tour lasted about 2 and ½ half hours and we walked about 2 miles, mostly uphill, in the down town area. It was so hot; we had to stop periodically in order to rest.

We walked on old cobblestone roads and through alleyways, past clubs and bars in Shockoe Bottom, and then continued on until we reached the heart of downtown where there were more corporate and Federal buildings.

One of the first haunted places we walked by was the Poe Museum. This was once the home of the famous Gothic novelist Edgar Allen Poe. I took pictures of this beautiful brick building but unfortunately I didn't get anything paranormal appearing in the photos.

We stopped at the site of the Governor's Mansion. This house is one of the state's finest Federal style buildings. When the mansion was first built, it was very plain and didn't have many furnishings. In time, a number of improvements were made to the house.

The mansion has been visited by five US Presidents, Winston Churchill, King Edward VII, Queen Mother of Elizabeth of England, Charles Lindburgh, and Admiral Richard E Byrd. Thomas Jefferson, James Monroe, William Henry Harrison, John Tyler and Patrick Henry have also lived there. In 1863, General Stonewall Jackson's body lay in state in the room downstairs in the mansion.

In the early 1890's, Governor Philip W. McKinney encountered an apparition of a beautiful young lady. He entered a bedroom and was startled to find a woman sitting in the windowsill. He quickly retreated to his wife's room to question who the visitor was. She replied that she didn't have any guests at the time. He then reentered his bedroom but the lady had vanished.

Another time, a Capital police officer saw a woman standing near the curtains of an upstairs bedroom. This was an area of the house that no unauthorized guests were allowed to go. He went upstairs to find out who she was and why she was there. When he approached her, she vanished before his eyes.

Security officers working in the house have heard footsteps, and a rustling sound of a gown in the hallway. One officer chased the sound into the basement. When he got there, the sound mysteriously stopped. Other employees have heard doors slam and someone walk upstairs when there is no one around.

In 1972, a hurricane traveled through Richmond, causing a blackout at the mansion. The whole house was dark except for a single light bulb in the stairwell of the house. There were no light switch's that would turn it off. Also during the blackout, something or someone moved several of the paintings in the Governor's room.

A Capital Hill policeman was in the basement one night and he felt something touch his face. He was so scared that he ran out of the house. He quit his job the following day. Another eerie occurrence reported was when another officer was down in the basement. He noticed the Governor's dog acting strange. The hair on its back was raised and he was barking at a window. He then felt a chill in the air. He noticed that the window was frosted over, although, it was in the middle of the summer. Then he saw the curtains moving. A few seconds later the curtains stopped. Then the frost on the window disappeared.

I took photos of a Federal building next to the Governor's Mansion on July 22, 2006. It was under renovation and there was a fence around it. I couldn't get very close to it. In the few photos that I took, streaks of light and vortexes appeared next to the fence.

Paranormal activity is usually peeked when buildings are under construction or renovation. All the energy surrounding the activity stirs up the restless spirit. They try to draw off this energy to manifest. Maybe they don't approve of the new modifications and they want the rooms or the structure of the building to remain in its original grandeur. Sometimes the spirits make their presence known. This could be what is appearing in the photos.

I have taken other pictures of similar activity when I photographed the original structure of The Witch Dungeon in Salem, Massachusetts. There are many vortexes surrounding this building when it was under construction.

There is no information on who haunts this Federal building or why. Could it be the beautiful woman who haunts the Governor's Mansion? Could she be wondering from the mansion to the building? Or could it be the land on which the structure was built on that is haunted?

Federal Building near the Governors Mansion
Richmond, Va. 7/2006

NEW MEXICO

ALBUQUERQUE - (OLD TOWN)

CHURCH STREET CAFÉ
2003

CASA DE RUIZ

The history of this quaint café in Old Town, Albuquerque, New Mexico is uncertain. Much has been lost with the passage of time. Casa de Ruiz, which means "The House of Ruiz", is the oldest residence in Albuquerque. It is also one of the oldest structures in the state of New Mexico.

This property was built by the Ruiz family in the early 1700's. Its last inhabitant was Ruffina G. Ruiz. She remained here until she died in 1991 at the age of 91. It is rumored that her mother Sarah, still haunts this dwelling. Since the early 18th century this house had never been sold and had remained in the Ruiz family. The Ruiz family was traced back to Julianna Lucero and Francisco Ruiz who were both born around 1834. They had a daughter named Sarah Ruiz who was born in 1880. She was Ruffian's mother.

According to the Sanborn maps, which were first used in 1891 by the Sanborn Insurance Company to estimate property values, the house was originally built in the hacienda style. This resembled the old classic Spanish "U-Shape". The house remained this way until 1920, when half of the house was destroyed by a flood.

The house was made of adobe brick called terrones. This type of brick was used when the area around Rio Grande River was a marshy swamp. In 1820, a drainage system for the swamp was installed. It wasn't until after 1820 that adobe bricks were made like they are today with a dryer mud. There is no longer a swampy area to make terrones. This confirms the antiquity of the house. Also the thickness of the walls is an indication of age. The thicker the adobe wall is, the older the structure. The walls are over two feet thick in some areas. They were built this thick because this material is cooler in the summer and warmer in the winter. Research on this house still continues today.

This house is now called the Church Street Café located in Old Town Albuquerque. Sarah's spirit is rumored to still haunt this restaurant. She lived in this house for many years. Sarah had a fiancé that treated her badly. They would get into terrible knife fights and roll around outside in the street fighting. When her finance found out she was pregnant, he left town suddenly. He didn't want anything to do with her or raising a child. Sarah was a headstrong, independent woman, who raised her daughter Ruffina, by herself. She owned the house and property which she inherited from her family. She vowed that she would stay there until the day she died.

Several years later, her ex-fiancé returned to see his daughter. He was married and had his own family. Sarah didn't want Ruffina associating with him. Ruffina got married and moved away but Sarah remained in the house until she died.

The house sat vacant for many years. It was finally sold. The new owner purchased it, planning to renovate it and turn it into a restaurant. She hired a contractor to do some of the work on the construction of the building. While he was working on the renovations, a woman appeared and ordered him to stop working and leave. He was packing up his tools when the owner approached him to ask why he was leaving. He was confused, and said another woman was here and asked him to stop the construction. He thought it was her business partner. She then replied "I don't have a partner; there is no-one here but us."

This was the beginning of the ghostly activity in the café. The woman that appeared to the contractor is believed to be the ghost of Sarah. She refuses to leave her house and doesn't want anybody changing the style or construction of the house.

There have been lights turning on and off, silverware re-arranged on the table, and strange sounds heard by the owner and employees of the café. One eerie incident that occurred was when a couple of people in the café heard a loud thud in the other room. It seemed to be coming from a glass display case. There was a nativity scence located inside the case. All of a sudden, one of the wise men was thrown against the inside of the glass case. When someone tried to place the figurine where he was before, the wise men was thrown around once again. For whatever reason, I guess the ghost of Sarah, doesn't like this statue. She could have just done this in order to scare people away and make her presence known.

Upon further research, it was discovered that the contractor was the grandson of the man that Sarah was engaged to. Was she trying to get revenge on her fiancé by scaring and harassing his grandson? Maybe he reminded her of her long ago lover who betrayed her and left her so long ago. One thing for sure, is that Sarah's spirit still walks the halls of the restaurant, thinking it is still her house. She refuses to leave. However, she is no threat to the owner or her staff. They actually acknowledge her presence and say goodnight to her everyday upon leaving.

When I was on the ghost tour, I captured a photo of a huge orb near the roof of the restaurant. It's probably Sarah looking down at everyone who comes through her door. Watching, waiting, and hoping her ex-fiancé comes through the door so she can seek her revenge.

Church Street Café
(Old Town) Albuquerque, NM. 6/2003

BEHIND PLAZA HACIENDA

(NEAR PASQUALE STREET)

In Old Town Albuquerque there is a sitting area behind a restaurant where I photographed some paranormal activity. At one time, this was a barn where secluded lovers would go. The barn used to be located next to a loud, rowdy bar that is no longer there.

The legend states that a woman walked past this area late one night and heard a rustling near a hay bail. When she checked to see what the sound was, she was astonished to find out that it was her fiancé in the arms of another woman. In a rage, she picked up what she could find laying around, which happened to be an axe.

She then proceeded to hack her fiancé to death with the axe. The woman ran away screaming in a frenzy.

Many years later, the crazy woman would chase any lovers that happened to come to this area late a night. It is not certain how many people she did kill. She was never caught. Her spirit supposedly haunts this area.

In June of 2003, I went on a ghost tour in Old Town and I was able to photograph some eerie vortexes in the area where the man was murdered. I was also there in October of 2006. Similar more prominent vortexes appeared in the same spot.

Sitting Area (behind Plaza Hacienda)
(Old Town) Albuquerque, NM. 10/2006
(Vortexes appear where the man was murdered)

COVERED WAGON & LA FIESTA RESTAURANT
2006

I photographed a building called the Covered Wagon on South Plaza Street in Old Town, Albuquerque New Mexico. This used to be an old brothel back in the early 1900s. Now there is a gift shop on the lower floor. When I developed the film, there appeared to be many vortexes on the balcony. This is where an apparition of a prostitute has been seen. She fell and broke her neck on the stairway leading to the balcony. Her ghost has been seen roaming the balcony and stairway late at night.

One night in particular, a police officer was called to investigate a naked woman walking around on the balcony of the covered wagon. Several eyewitnesses saw her. She was shouting crude remarks at the people who passed by on the street below. She tried to lure some men upstairs.

When the officer arrived, he saw the woman and told her to come down from the balcony. He tried to persuade her to put on some clothing. She looked over at him and then suddenly ran towards the staircase and vanished. He couldn't believe his eyes. Some people have reported that they felt like they were being pushed down the stairs in the same area leading to the balcony. When they turned around no- one was there.

Also on this street, just a few buildings down is a restaurant called "Casa de fiesta." Some strange paranormal activity has been witnessed by some of the waiters and bartenders who work there. Tables and chairs have been moved around when there is no one in the restaurant. The staff will find things in disarray the next morning. Strange noises have been heard in many areas throughout the building. A lot of activity seemed to come from the basement area.

Many years ago during reconstruction of the building a secret underground passageway was discovered. It leads to another restaurant on the corner, known as La Placita. These two restaurants used to be houses back in the early 1800's. This passageway was built for the women and children to hideout during the Indian raids.

The secret door to the basement would open and close on its own. Some of the waiters would hear pounding on the inside of the door after hours. It sounded like someone was trying to get out. They could hear screams and crying as if someone was trapped in the basement. Could this be the ghosts of the local residents that were killed in the Indian raids?

Eerie vortexes appear in the photos of this historic restaurant.

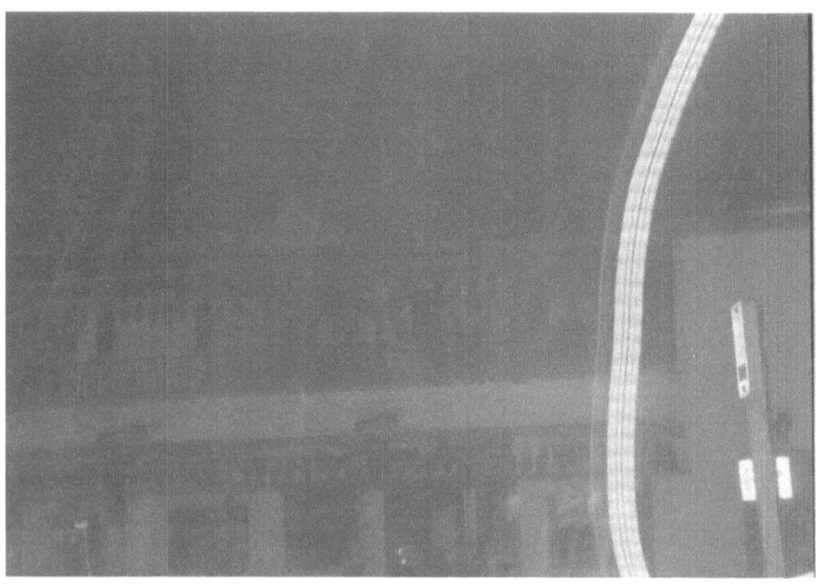

Covered Wagon
(Old Town) Albuquerque, NM. 10/2006

Covered Wagon
(Old Town) Albuquerque, NM. 10/2006

BASKETSHOP
2006

The Basket-Shop is a huge souvenir shop in Old Town. This building is also haunted. There is not much information about who haunts this building or why. I have photographed the store window at night and have gotten two white streaks of light coming out of the main doorway as well as activity inside the store. This looks like the same kind of paranormal activity that I discovered in other haunted buildings around Old Town.

This basket shop is very close to the plaza that has a high concentration of paranormal activity. The Plaza is located on the land where a cemetery once was. This area flooded and the bodies were relocated across the street. Several (EVPS) Electronic Voice Phenomenon, have been recorded here.

I wonder if the spirits walk back and forth from building to building. This may be what this photo suggests. They may haunt several locations not just one, especially if they are bound to the land. I must be able to pick up on their energy, because when I feel like something is there, I take a picture and usually something paranormal appears in the photo.

Basketshop
(Old Town) Albuquerque, NM. 10/2006

SAINTS & MARTYRS
2006

This is an unusual shop in the heart of Old Town. It is located next to Our Lady of Guadalupe Chapel. It has an impressive collection of museum quality antiques, religious paintings, statues, crucifixes and rosaries. Many of these items are imported from Europe and Mexico. A lot of the items are of southwestern style and origin. The shop also carries books, periodicals and newly-manufactured items.

This is one of the scariest stores I have ever stepped foot in. I discovered this shop when I first moved to New Mexico. I took some pictures at night, the week before I actually went on the ghost tour. I didn't know that this was one of the haunted locations on the tour. I just felt like something was drawing me to this shop.

As soon as I entered the store, I had an uneasy feeling. The air was thick and it was very hard to breathe. I had an instant feeling of dread and I felt like someone was behind me, watching my every move. I quickly turned around and saw a clown sign painted on a huge chunk of wood. It seemed to be staring back at me. I continued to walk deeper into the store examining the religious statues. I had an overwhelming feeling of genuine fear and I started feeling dizzy and nauseous. I could sense an evil presence lurking in the building. I firmly believe in haunted possessions, and I felt like some of these items could be cursed or possibly an evil spirit may inhabit them. I immediately left the shop.

As soon as I stepped outside the building, I felt better. The only other time I have ever sensed something of this caliber was when I walked into an antique bookstore in Salem, Massachusetts. This experience felt identical. The thick air and the evil presence permeated the air.

I came back to Saints and Martyrs one night in October and snapped a few photos in front of the store. When I developed the pictures, there were streaks of light or vortexes, indicating paranormal activity. During the ghost tour, we stopped in front of this building. The guide said that there have been sightings of a ghost roaming Old Town. This is one of the locations where he has been sited. Not much is known about his identity. He is described as looking like a western cowboy gunslinger. He has the 10-gallon hat and chaps and he is carrying a gun. His face appears to be a skeleton. The legend states that he is searching for his stolen fortune that he hid away many years ago. The first sighting of his ghost was in front of Saints and Martyrs. This is exactly the same spot that I photographed and got an anomaly in the photograph.

I took another picture in the alleyway next to Saints and Martyrs. This small area has various shops and is called Patio Escondido. It is on San Felipe Street. There were several vortexes also in this area. This could be evidence of the gunslinger ghost that lingers near Saints and Martyrs or several other ghosts that inhabit Old Town. This is an area where I felt a strong presence and when I turned around, I started snapping pictures.

Another area that is haunted is a parking lot near Hacienda Plaza. It is on the corner of Pasquale Avenue & Old Town Road. It is near Alfredo's Restaurant. I took a photograph there and got the same kind of vortexes appearing. This is where the first sighting of the gunslinger ghost appeared. Someone reported seeing what looked like an apparition of a skeletal cowboy hunched over grabbing his stomach. The legend states this is possibly the exact spot that the gold robber was shot and killed. The scene seems to replay over and over again indicating a residual haunting. The apparition is acting out his deadly gunfight in this exact spot.

Saints & Martyrs
(Old Town) Albuquerque, NM. 10/2006
(Strange vortexes appear where the gunslinger has been sighted)

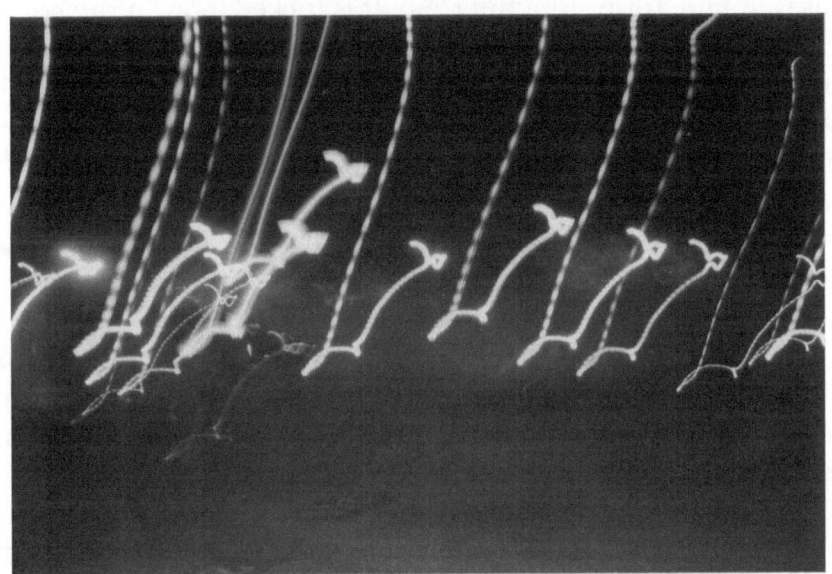

Parking lot near Hacienda Plaza
(Old Town) Albuquerque, NM. 0/2006
(This is the location of the first sighting of the gunslinger)

OUR LADY OF GUADALUPE CHAPEL
2006

The tiny Chapel of Our Lady of Guadalupe was erected in 1975. It was designed and built by Sister Giotto. It is haunted by an apparition of a lady in black. She has been seen on the far right bench, weeping. She wears a long black dress and a dark veil. It is suspected that the woman cries for the victims of the TWA flight 260.

On February 19, 1955, the plane crashed into the Sandia Mountains . It killed thirteen passengers and three crew members that were on board. The apparition has also been seen to enter the alleys that lead to the capilla only on the anniversary of the crash. Another theory is that the ghost only appears in times of tragedy such as a fatal crash on the interstate or some other disaster.

Our Lady of Guadalupe Chapel is located on San Felipe Street. This is in Old Town, Albuquerque. It is tucked away in the corner of Patio Escondido. It is opened 24hrs every day. There are many candles burning and flowers and gifts that align the altar. The many people that visit the Chapel throughout the year bring these offerings. The eerie thing about the chapel is the doors are always open and cannot close. I've visited several times and I always get lost trying to find this small building. It is located far down an alleyway. If you are not sure exactly where it is, it is easy to get lost trying to find it.

The last time I was there, as I was leaving, I remember firmly closing the door behind me. All of a sudden, it flew open, and started banging in the breeze. I quickly turned around and didn't see anything. I felt a little uneasy so I left immediately.

The first time I visited this Chapel, I could feel a strong presence as I entered the room. As I approached the altar it seemed to get stronger and stronger. I walked away to photograph the beautiful wood- carved chairs. It was very dark inside this room with a little candlelight illuminating. I decided to take a picture where I felt the presence the strongest at that time. What appeared in my photo was a green vortex coming out of one of the chairs.

This energy may indicate the lady in black sitting in this chair. The feeling of someone else in this room intensified so much that I had to leave the chapel and go outside to get some fresh air.

The legend states that the lady in black may have been a holy woman that perished in the crash and her ghost wanders this area. She is looking for anyone who may have survived the crash or injured passengers so that she can help them. She may not know that she has passed on. It could be her spirit that walks in and out of this chapel opening and closing the doors.

Inside Our Lady of Guadalupe Chapel
(Old Town) Albuquerque, NM. 10/2006
(Green vortex emanated from the chair)

Our Lady of Guadalupe Chapel
(Old Town) Albuquerque, NM. 10/2006
(Alleyway to Chapel)

LA PLACITA RESTAURANT
2006

I have taken the Old Town Ghost Tour twice, once in June 2003 and in October 2006. Both times, I have captured on film, strong compelling evidence of paranormal activity. Strange vortexes appear in all the pictures of the La Placita Restaurant. This is probably due to the many spirits that inhabit the building. It is incredible how haunted this part of Old Town, Albuquerque is. This was definitely one of the scarier tours that I have been on. The Gettysburg tour was probably the scariest tour and this one would take second place. When you are walking around the plaza at night, it feels very spooky. The air feels charged with electricity and you feel like someone is watching you from the old buildings around town. There is a thick heaviness in the air. Almost every restaurant or store is haunted.

The La Placita Restaurant is also known as Casa de Armijo. In 1706, El Colorado Don Juan Armijo Maestas constructed this adobe building. It was then sold to Ambrosio Armijo. It was originally built for defense against raiding by Nomadic Native Americans. It was a fort and a refuge. Then it became a trading post.

In 1930, the building was restored and remolded in its original grandeur of the 1700's. This is the only building in Albuquerque that has an intact placita (indoor patio). The staircase was imported from Spain in 1883.

Four spirits haunt this restaurant. They are Victoria, a little girl who lived there at one time, Elizabeth, a woman who has not been identified, George, who is a mischievous ghost, and an unnamed spirit who haunts one of the rooms upstairs.

The most reported phenomenon is in the women's restroom and the upstairs area.

Victoria is believed to be a servant girl who died in 1783 of tuberculosis. Witnesses describe her as having long black hair and wearing a beautiful beaded white dress. She appears as a solid person then she disappears through a wall or suddenly vanishes in the hallway. She mostly appears in front of other children or the elderly. She sometimes appears in the mirror in the women's restroom. This was once Victoria's bedroom. It is located in the hallway behind the staircase. She likes to pull on the skirts of the waitress's and patrons to get their attention. Victoria has been sighted by several people taking the Old Town ghost tour.

Another spirit that roams the restaurant is named George. He likes to mimic voices. He has been known to go behind employees and whisper their names. When they turn around no one is there.

Another ghost that has been reported throughout the building is named Elizabeth. Her identity is unknown. She is never sighted alone. She always appears with the ghost of the little girl- Victoria. She is usually seen near the antique stairs. Some people believe she may be the daughter of the man who had the stairs erected. He bought these steps as a wedding gift for his daughter. She was married at the base of these steps. Her wedding train was almost 30 feet long and extended to the top of the stairs.

One night a security guard was making his rounds in Old Town. He glanced over at the restaurant and saw through the window, a woman holding a baby. She turned and looked directly at him then vanished into thin air.

Lastly, there is a ghost that lingers in the room upstairs across from the manager's office. This room is now used as a storage area. This unfriendly spirit is unidentified and dislikes women. Several cold spots can be felt in this upstairs area. Female workers do not like to go upstairs alone for fear of being touched or grabbed. Usually they send the male workers upstairs to get their supplies from the storage area.

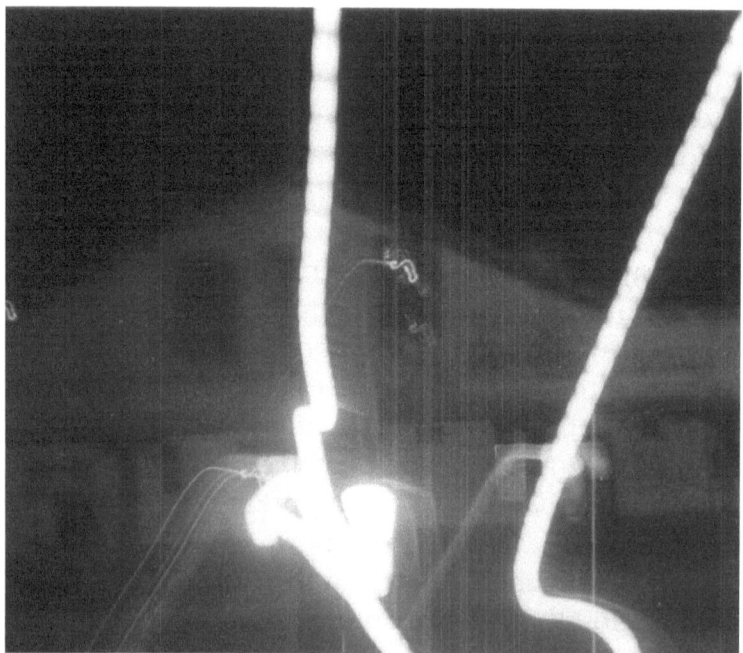

La Placita Restaurant
(Old Town) Albuquerque, NM. 10/2006
(Powerful vortexes in front of the restaurant)

La Placita Restaurant
(Old Town) Albuquerque, NM. 10/2006

PLAZA DON LUIS
2007

The area that is known today as Plaza Don Luis is located on Romero Street in Old Town, Albuquerque, New Mexico. This little area is very active with paranormal energy. There have been several EVPS (Electronic Voice Phenomenon) collected around the area where there is a huge water fountain. No one knows whom these disembodied voices belong to, but they are quite eerie. The plaza has brick walkways surrounded by various shops and a huge staircase leading upstairs to more shops.

I took several pictures here in October of 2007, when I went on the ghost tour of Old Town. I saw paranormal activity in almost all of the pictures that I had taken that night.

At one time in the 1800s, a church stood on this land that is now the plaza. A graveyard was located behind the church. There was a major flood and the church was destroyed and washed away. The graveyard was also destroyed. Many corpses and coffins had risen from beneath the ground to the surface and were washed away in the raging water. Some of the coffins and bodies ended up across the street, where the San Felipe Church is now located. Due to the flood, the church was rebuilt and moved to this new location which is now called the San Felipe de Neri Church. Some bodies still remain underneath this church.

After the water resided from the flood, many of the remaining coffins were dug up and relocated. However, due to the flooding, not all of the caskets remained intact. Many body parts were separated by the water. Some limbs were washed away while other parts remained underground. It was really hard to distinguish who was missing from the cemetery and who remained buried there. There are two coffins that remain buried underneath the floor of one of the art stores in the plaza. This store is the Andrew Pueblo Pottery. These coffins cannot be removed; otherwise the foundation of the floor will collapse.

The stores, staircase, and water fountain were built over the cemetery. This could be why the area is so haunted.

When I took a picture of the stairway, strange white vortexes appeared in my photo. You can barely see the stairway. Also, if you look closely at the picture of the Andrew Pueblo Pottery store; you can see a weird shape in the window. It almost looks like a small face peering out. I took two photos of this window. In the first picture everything appears normal. In the second picture, which was only taken seconds later, a face appears.

Andrew Pueblo Pottery
(Old Town) Albuquerque, NM. 10/2007
(It looks like a face in right corner above the bench)

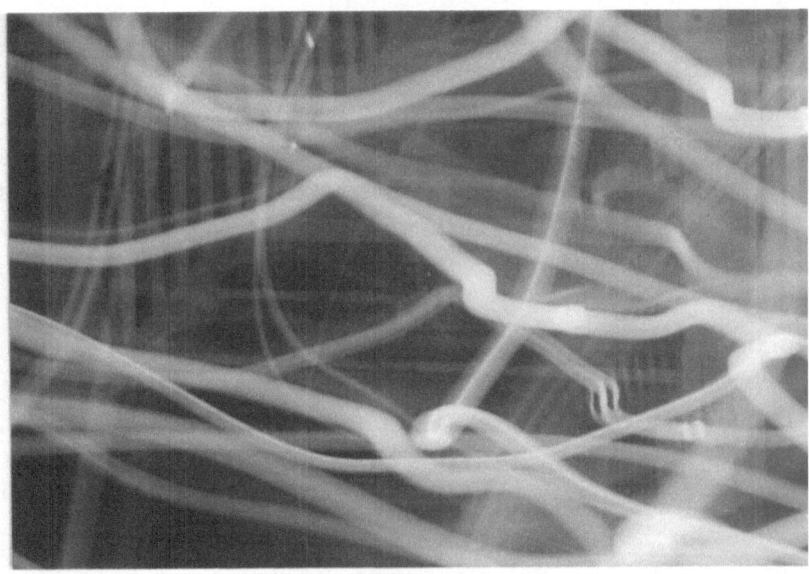

Staircase in the Don Luis Plaza
(Old Town) Albuquerque, NM. 10/2007
(Strange white vortexes)

ALBUQUERQUE (DOWNTOWN)

ALBUQUERQUE PRESS CLUB (WHITTLESEY HOUSE)
2007

The Albuquerque Press Club is located behind the Memorial Hospital up on a small hill next to Highland Park. This hospital was a mental facility at one time. Architect, Charles Whittlesey built and designed this log house. It was his family residence in 1903.

It has a three- story frame structure that was designed after a Norwegian villa. It has low pitch roofs with exposed log fronting; rough log- cut facades and a wide porch.

Since the house is located on Highland Hill, it has a beautiful view of the Sandias in the east and the river in the west. The view was unobstructed at one time due to very little vegetation or trees. Albuquerque wasn't built up yet, so there weren't many buildings nearby. Now the view is a street, a highway and some trees in the park.

In 1908, Whittleseley sold the house to Theodore S. Woolsey Jr., who owned it for twelve years. He added on an addition to the south side of the house and framed out the northwest corner of the main porch. In 1916, he then leased it to Mr. Andros, who was the President of Whitney Hardware.

The head nurse at the Albuquerque Sanitarium (Memorial Hospital); would walk past this house everyday and admire its beauty. She convinced her boyfriend that if he would buy it for her she would marry him. Her name was Clifford Hall. He bought the house, they got married, and she lived there for the next forty years. During this time, the house went through extensive remodeling and changes to the interior's design. Her personal life however was very turbulent. She was married and divorced twice. In order to make extra money; she rented out portions of the house.

The Highland Park "log" house, as it was known, was a showplace during the Thirties, Forties, and Fifties, where many wealthy people visited. Clifford loved her house and spent a great deal of time there and in its surroundings.

Due to her age, the upkeep of the house was becoming too much for her. In 1960, she sold the house. A local Albuquerque fraternity purchased the house. They only had it for a few years. In 1966, they sold it because the fraternity moved closer to "The University of New Mexico." A man named John T Roberson leased it for the next several years. In the 1970's the Albuquerque Press Club eventually purchased it. They still own it today.

A weird thing that happened to me was when I moved to Albuquerque about three years ago. I wasn't familiar with the freeway yet and I would always get lost at the same exit where the Memorial Hospital and the Albuquerque Press Club is located. I remember looking at this huge abandoned building thinking to myself it definitely looks haunted. I would get an eerie feeling when I passed by it. I never knew the log house was behind it. It was almost as if something was drawing me to this haunted place. For months, I would get lost on the freeway and always end up there in front of the building. I decided to do some research and found some information from local authors that both places were haunted. So that's when I decided to go there at night and see if I could get some paranormal photos.

According to many eyewitnesses, the bar area has the highest level of activity. Faint sounds of a woman walking in high heels on a wooden floor have been heard near this area as well as other strange unexplainable noises. A shadowy image of a woman dressed in black dress was also seen at this location. Another incident that happened here was when a woman was working at the bar. She glanced over and saw a woman walk across the room and then disappear near the wall.

Many people who work at the Albuquerque Press Club think this woman is the ghost of Clifford Hall. Sometimes the bartenders leave a shot of gin for her at the bar at the end of the night. When they come in the next day, sometimes it is gone and sometimes it still remains there. I guess the ghost has to be in the mood to drink. It's a nice gesture anyway. It shows respect to the lady of the house.

There has also been activity reported near the pool table. The sound of pool balls moving around have been heard. In certain areas, near the pool table cold spots are felt, feelings of being watched are prevalent and a distinct smell of roses permeate the air.

The Memorial Hospital, which sits in front of the house, also has some reported strange paranormal activity. An apparition of a woman dressed in 1930's clothing, possibly a nurse, has been seen through the windows moving from room to room. Perhaps this is the ghost of Clifford Hall checking on the patients. She could be haunting the house as well as the hospital where she worked. It seems she refuses to leave the house that she loved so much.

I have photographed The Albuquerque Press Club several times at night and have never gotten anything unusual. I have even gone during a full moon, hoping the energy in the air would be stronger; therefore I would have a higher chance in photographing something paranormal. In this case, I had no luck. I decided to go in the daytime to get a better look at this beautiful house and take some photos.

The club was closed, so I took a look around the property and peeked in the windows. I was standing on the porch looking through the side window when I noticed a slight white mist hovering around the bookshelves. This room looks like a library. There is old furniture, wood walls, and a lot of books on the shelves. The woodwork is beautiful, so I asked my friend to take a picture through the window with her digital camera. A digital camera can take pretty clear pictures through glass unlike my 35mm, which would reflect the light off the window and ruin the picture.

When she downloaded the pictures on the computer she noticed a strange green anomaly, like a streak of light or vortex in front of the window. It was almost as if someone or something was standing right in front of us looking out the window in our direction. This is also the area where I saw the strange mist. This just reiterates that sometimes when you are looking for a spirit, you may not find one, but when you least expect it, then it will appear. Sometimes a spirit only shows itself when it wants to. I have investigated many places that claim to be haunted and highly active and I haven't gotten any physical evidence to prove the haunting. That doesn't mean the place is not haunted, it just means that there was no paranormal activity at the time I was there. Perhaps the spirit wasn't strong enough to manifest itself.

As I was writing this story for the book, another strange thing happened. When I left work that day I was stuck in traffic. The freeway was closed so I took an alternative way home. That road was also jam packed with traffic, so I decided to go to another road that ran parallel to the freeway. It was on the same road that the Memorial Hospital is located. I was stuck in bumper to bumper traffic right in front of the hospital. I felt a little spooked out because I had just been writing about this place a few hours ago. Once again, I felt that something was drawing me to this area. The spirits must know I am a true believer in the paranormal and it wants to get my attention for some reason.

Albuquerque Press Club
Downtown, Albuquerque, NM. 5/200
(Green vortex in front of the window)

CORRALES
2007

RANCHO DE CORRALES

The Rancho De Corrales is an ancient hacienda built in 1801 by Diego Montoya. It has been a restaurant for several decades. It was formerly known as the Territorial House.

Luis and Louisa Emberto purchased it in 1883. Both were known to have lovers. One night, they were having a social gathering. Their son killed a woman who he believed was his father's mistress. Luis moved out after the incident and threatened to kill his wife and her lover as well. He blamed her for convincing their son to murder the woman he was having an affair with.

On April 1898, Luis fired his gun twice, killing his wife. Then he fled into the night. The next morning, an armed posse gunned him down. They cornered Luis in a patch of trees not far from his home. Some people believe the posse was hired by his son. Due to the scandalous nature surrounding their deaths, neither Luis nor Louisa was allowed to be buried on consecrated ground. They were entombed in unmarked graves on their property. The graves are located across the irrigation ditch, to the west of the restaurant. Their presence is still felt here today. The exact location of the graves is unknown.

There are huge mulberry trees in front of the building. Many years ago, these trees were used to hang cattle thieves and other criminals. In October 1975, this building was known as the Territorial House. During a bloody battle, two armed thugs died of gunshot wounds. One previous owner died from a heart attack in the building and another owner suffered multiple bullet wounds but survived. A lot of this bloodshed occurred where the bar is now located. There are still visible bullet holes in the walls.

In 1987, the business was bought and the name changed to Rancho De Corrales. A lot of paranormal activity has been reported in this building. The most active time is from midnight to three in the morning. The areas that experience activity are the banquet room and the bar. This coincides with where some of the murders have taken place.

A staff member claims that she left the banquet room only for a few moments, when she returned, all the chairs had been placed on top of the tables. There weren't any customers in the restaurant and she was alone. Another person said he saw an apparition of and old man sitting near the fireplace rocking back and forth in a chair. He was in the dark and when the light was turned on, he vanished. Other employee's have seen a woman wearing a white flowing gown sitting on a barstool. When she is approached, she suddenly disappears into thin air. The sightings are only for a few seconds at a time.

In the bar, the heavy cooler doors have been seen opening and closing on their own. Faucets in the bathroom mysteriously turn on. An apparition of a woman wearing a Victorian style dress appeared to an employee. She walked into the bathroom and disappeared. In the middle of the night another employee saw a glow of a ghostly cigarette moving through the air. Ghostly voices and a child crying have been heard in the bar area early in the morning, when no one else is in the building but a solitary employee.

I traveled to this restaurant one night during a full moon. It was around 9:00pm. The employees were getting ready to close the building for the night. They looked at me briefly, and then continued their business. I wasn't sure if I was allowed to be on the property. Currently, I think this restaurant is only open for private banquets. I didn't want them to see me snooping around taking pictures. They would probably think I was crazy, but I was very serious about getting a paranormal photograph that night. I snapped a couple of pictures in the front of the building near the big tree, and a few around the side of the building where the bar is located.

When I developed the film, there was a huge orb in the air overlooking the area where the hanging tree was located. Could this also be the area where Luis and Louisa were buried? Are they still haunting this property? Or could this be the lost souls of the cattle thieves that were hung on the property?

Rancho De Corrales
Corrales, NM. 10/2007
(Large orb near hanging tree)

MESILLA
2007

THE PLAZA

When Mesilla was founded, the town's population was centered on the Plaza for defense against Apache raiders who were a constant threat to the settlement. The adobe buildings that were built then still remain standing today.

In 1853, the most historic event was the Gadsden Purchase. Troops from Ft. Fillmore raised the United States flag in the Mesilla Plaza.

In 1871, there was a political riot. After political rallies, Republicans and Democrats met on the West Side of the Plaza. Fighting occurred resulting in several deaths and injuries.

In 1957, Mesilla Plaza was declared a state monument of New Mexico. In 1982, it was listed on the National Register as a National Historic landmark. The historic district was added to the National Registry in 1985. Today, the Plaza has gift shops, galleries, world- renowned dining, drinking establishments, and historical buildings.

In 1978, the plaza and gazebo were refurbished. The Plaza is also home to many cultural and historical activities.

I took several photos of the Plaza at night, which included the beautiful church, the gazebo, La Posta Restaurant, the Double Eagle Restaurant, and many of the surrounding shops. One building on the corner looked like a big warehouse. It appeared to be vacant and as I approached it, it looked very spooky. There wasn't any business name on the brick building. For some reason,

I was drawn to this building. The whole Plaza felt very eerie at night. There was an intense feeling in the air.

I took a few pictures of this abandoned building, and sure enough, there were vortexes appearing around this area. I'm not sure who haunts this building.

There is a haunted restaurant called the Double Eagle that is across the street very close to the vicinity of this building. This was a family residence at one time. The first owners of the house were the Maes family. They were in the import-export business. The mother was a very proud woman. Her family had prestige, power, and connections. Her grand plans centered on her eldest son Armando. She wanted him to marry into aristocracy in Mexico City. However, Armando was in love with a servant girl named Inez. The mother did not approve of this union.

In a fit of rage, she stabbed Inez in the chest. Armando rushed to shield the attack and was also stabbed in the back. He died three days later. His mother did not speak from that day forward. She was so ashamed and grief stricken that she killed her son. Her last spoken word was her dying son's name.

The legend states that the young lover's spirits inhabit the Carlotta Salon, in the Double Eagle Restaurant. This area was formerly Armando's bedroom. The ghostly occurrences are quite active today. There have been reports of tables that have been left in one spot, mysteriously found in a different place the next morning. Wineglasses have been broken, and whispered names and the scent of perfume have also been reported.

The most compelling reports are of two over-stuffed master and mistress chairs in the corner of the Salon. The chairs have been newly re-upholstered but show signs of wear and tear. However, the velvet fabric is worn in the shape of two human bodies. It's almost as if two people have been sitting in the chairs.

Since the Plaza has so much history, it is hard to determine the exact spirit haunting the buildings and the Plaza.

Could it be Armando and Inez haunting these streets? Or could it be the several people that died in 1871 due to the political riot? Or perhaps this land may be haunted by the many Mexican troops that were garrisoned in Mesilla in 1846?

Abandoned building located in The Plaza.
Mesilla, NM. 4/2007
(Vortex appearing on the right side of the photo)

NEVADA

LAS VEGAS
2007

CARLUCCIO TIVIOLI GARDENS

My friend and I went on the haunted Las Vegas Tour October 20, 2007. We got on a bus that took us to several haunted locations throughout Las Vegas and the surrounding areas. One of the last stops on the tour was the Carluccio Tivoli Gardens Restaurant. This is across the parking lot from the Liberace Museum.

We got off the bus and walked around the outside of the building. I took several photos. When I developed the pictures, I got some amazing results. One photo in particular, is similar to the picture I took at the House of Seven Gables. It appears very red and smudged. There are some very strange red bands of light that look like they are forming into the shape of a piano. It looks like something is moving at high speed. Could this be Liberace trying to manifest himself along with his piano, using the energy from the neon signs? The night was very clear and all the other photos came out normal.

Liberace had many homes, but the one that he enjoyed the most was in a quiet, suburban neighborhood in Las Vegas. It is only a few blocks over from his famous restaurant. The house didn't look very glamorous from the outside, but it is very extravagant inside according to some of the pictures on display in his museum. Liberace was very active in his local community and supported many of the fundraisers and charities.

The tour guide mentioned an eerie occurrence that happened a few days prior to the ghost tour. The power went off in all the houses in Liberace's neighborhood, including his for a few days. Finally the power came back on, in all the homes on his side of the street, except for his house which remained in the dark. The power had not been restored in his house yet on the night we past by it. The guide told us that the electric company had been working on it, but they couldn't figure out why the power didn't come back on. Even the house next to him and across the street had electricity.

The strange thing about this incident was that it happened around the anniversary of his death.

Carlucci Tivioli Gardens is an Italian Restaurant that was owned by Liberace. This was one of Liberace's dreams; to own a restaurant. He loved to cook and even wrote a few cookbooks. He purchased it in 1982 and renamed it Liberace Tivoli Gardens. He did most of the interior decorating himself. In the piano room, there is sparkling overhead lighting and mirrored walls. He imported the woodwork in the English Lounge from a pub in London.

Liberace was a hands on owner. He would over-see menu planning. Many times he would quietly slip into the main dining area and play piano for the people in the restaurant. He would also play for his friends, Dolly Pardon and Debbie Reynolds, when they were in town performing. Sometimes Liberace would drop in the restaurant after he performed in one of the large showrooms on the strip. Many people have reported seeing Liberace's apparition in the piano lounge, or standing near a window in the restaurant.

One employee saw the reflection of a rhinestone-covered cape while he was cleaning a mirror in the piano lounge. He turned around but no one was there. Other employees have heard glasses clinking together and silverware being moved around.

The employee who spotted the cape in the mirror saw the exact rhinestone cape in the Liberace museum many weeks later. There have been many electrical disturbances throughout the restaurant. There is a lot of activity in the ladies bathroom. People have reported seeing doors lock and unlock, and water faucets turning on and off by themselves. Orbs have shown up in some photographs that were taken in these areas of the bathroom.

One night, on the anniversary of Liberace's death, the power went off in the entire restaurant. Wine and beer bottles toppled over and spilled out all over the bar. An employee remembered it was his birthday and the staff sang "Happy Birthday" to Liberace. Suddenly, the lights went back on and the bottles stopped falling. It seemed that his spirit just wanted a little recognition. He didn't want to be forgotten.

Liberace was born May 16, 1919. He was the survivor of twins. Liberace died February 4, 1987 due to complications from Aids.

He was a national icon. Liberace was the highest paid pianist ever and was known worldwide as "Mr. Showmanship". He was known for his joyful music, glittering costumes, candelabra, charisma, diamonds, and humor. He had many cars, pianos, and homes.

Over the years, Liberace acquired many prestigious awards. They were: Instrumentalist of the Year, Best Dressed Entertainer, and Entertainer of the Year. He also earned two Emmy Awards, six gold albums, and two stars on the Hollywood Walk of Fame.

In 1977, he founded the non- profit Liberace Foundation for the Performing and Creative Arts.

Liberace opened his famous Museum in Las Vegas, Nevada on April 15, 1979. This museum serves as the key funding arm for the Foundation.

In October of 2007, I visited the Liberace Museum. It had a very impressive collection of cars and a variety of unique pianos. What I enjoyed the most was the separate building that has on display many of Liberace's extravagant outfits.

It's amazing to imagine that Liberace's ghost is still haunting the restaurant and the museum. He still has a desire to entertain people from beyond the grave.

Carluccio Tivioli Gardens
Las Vegas, NV. 10/2007
(Intense red vortexes)

FLAMINGO HOTEL

At one time famous gangsters flocked to Las Vegas, Nevada. Benjamin "Bugsy" Siegel saw the potential of this gambling Mecca. In 1946, he persuaded his Mafia bosses to invest and build the most luxurious hotel and casino. It cost three times more then the original estimate to build the Flamingo Hotel. Unfortunately the casino was a flop. The Flamingo eventually started to turn a profit, but the Mafia bosses found out that Bugsy embezzled money in order to build it.

The hotel had 77 rooms, which were very plush for that time. Bugsy's room or "The Presidential Suite" was built especially for his needs. The windowpanes were bulletproof. There was only one entrance to the top floor suite, but there were five exits. There was a hidden ladder leading from the hallway closet to the basement tunnel, which led into the underground tunnel. There was a chauffeured getaway car waiting there at all times.

On June 20, 1947, Bugsy was shot once in the head and four times in his stomach. His girlfriend was Virginia Hill. He was killed in her mansion.

In 1993, the final wall of the Pink Flamingo was torn down. A new luxurious hotel was built in its place. It contained many upscale restaurants and a huge casino floor. The only thing that originally remains from Bugsy is a plaque in the Rose Garden.

Wandering paths and beautiful gardens were built many years later. Swans, waterfalls, birds, roses, and brightly colored koi fish surround the area where Bugsy's ghost has been seen. His apparition has been spotted near the monument dedicated to him, the pool, the wedding chapel, and the Presidential Suite of the old Flamingo Hotel. Since his room was torn down, his spirit has now been sighted in the penthouse of the Presidential Suite of the new hotel.

There have been many sightings of Bugsy's smiling phantom. He is neatly dressed in a smoking jacket and slacks of the 1940's. Even though he was killed in Beverly Hills, Ca, his spirit seems to be linked to this place. The Flamingo was Buggy's dream casino and hotel. This is probably where he was the happiest. His spirit may still be overseeing the casino and not want to cross over to the other side.

This is one of the stops on the haunted bus tour that I took on October 20, 2007. We were able to get off the bus and walk through part of the hotel into the beautiful outdoor garden area. We walked over to Bugsy Siegel's Monument and I took a couple of pictures. I also photographed the waterfall that is surrounded by flamingos and a doorway leading to the Presidential Suite.

In all three areas, some strange anomaly appeared in each one of the pictures. The picture of the Suite showed a burning outline around the doorway. The monument looked a little fuzzy and almost as if was moving. The most impressive photo was the one of the waterfall.

Vortexes appear shooting out of the waterfall and around it. Could this be the area where Bugsy was standing that night I was there? He could have been trying to manifest himself to prove that he still exists and is lingering around the hotel.

Flamingo Hotel
(Bugsy's apparition has been seen in this doorway -Presidential Suite)
Las Vegas, NV. 10/2007

Flamingo Hotel
(Vortexes surrounding small water fountain in the courtyard)
Las Vegas, NV. 10/2007

HENDERSON
2007

FOXRIDGE PARK

Another stop on the haunted Vegas tour was Foxridge Park. It is located on the outskirts of Las Vegas, in the small town of Henderson at 420 Valle Verde Road. It was about a 20 minute bus ride to get there. We arrived at Foxridge Park at 10:30pm. Everyone was able to get off the bus and walk around the park and take photographs.

The tour guide gave us all dowsing rods. We were instructed how to use these. The guide showed us the primary areas where the most energy was concentrated. These are the places where there have been the highest levels of paranormal activity recorded. Some people have seen orbs, bright lights, and apparitions. The spirits seem to be drawn to these high-energy fields.

The areas I got the most spirit activity were near the tree and the picnic table. This is where three ghosts have been spotted and remain lingering. Two of the spirits were teenage boys that are mostly seen sitting together on the picnic table near the trash can. The other spirit is a woman who is seen alone, near the large tree. When I was walking through with my dowsing rods, they were swinging backwards and as I got closer to the haunted areas, they were crossing over each other. This usually indicates there is energy which can be paranormal in nature.

No one knows the origins of these spirits or why they haunt this particular park. When I photographed the picnic table, I caught on film, two light streaks forming next to each other. The boys have been seen in this vicinity. When I took a picture of the tree, there was one single light streak in front of it. Perhaps this is the ghost of the woman often seen walking around at night. Her apparition has been spotted near this tree.

The forth ghost that haunts the park is probably the most well known. He has been seen haunting this place for years. Perhaps this is because he was struck down by a car on the bordering road. He is usually sighted playing by the swings between 1:00am - 3:00am. Some people have reported hearing a child singing near the swing set late at night. One evening a man saw an apparition of the boy on the swing. He looked over at the boy and his face distorted and became demonic looking, then after a few moments the child disappeared.

Some ghost hunters have taken pictures and received compelling photos of this boy. The most extraordinary picture I saw of the boy was from the waist down. You cannot see his upper body in the photo, only his legs and feet. He appears to be walking. This photo is similar to the apparition I saw in Gettysburg a year before.

I was not able to photograph this area of the park when I was on the Haunted Vegas tour, due to respect for his family. They live nearby and still mourn his death. They asked if the people from the ghost tour could refrain from disturbing the area where he still haunts. There is a little memorial there in his honor.

It is a public park, and we could have gone back afterwards, but it was so dark that night, and I was unfamiliar with the roads. I thought I would get lost. There are no streetlights there and we were not sure exactly where we were going. I hope to get back to this park in the near future for a further investigation.

Foxridge Park
Henderson, NV. 10/2007
(Vortexes near the tree- apparition of a woman has been seen here)

Foxridge Park
Henderson, NV. 10/2007
(Vortexes near the picnic table- apparitions of two young boys were seen here)

Foxridge Park
Henderson, NV. 10/2007
(Vortexes near the picnic table- apparitions of two young boys were seen here)

Foxridge Park
Henderson, NV. 10/2007
(People from the ghost tour picking up energy from the dowsing rods)
(Vortexes appearing where the apparitions of two young boys have been seen)

COLORADO

ESTES PARK
2008

THE STANLEY HOTEL

I arrived at Estes Park in the early afternoon for the Stanley Hotel ghost tour. The temperature was in the 60's and it was a little overcast and cloudy. I was excited to go on the ghost tour that evening. I heard a lot of stories about this famous hotel and I couldn't wait to see it. Our tour guide was very informative. I decided to tape-record the tour, so if I got any paranormal photos, I could pinpoint exactly where they were taken and I would have the accurate story to correspond with that photo.

I took many pictures of the haunted hot spots, but I didn't get anything unusual in the photos. I was very disappointed until I got home and reviewed the digital tape recorder. I got a very distinct EVP saying either 'A CAR' or 'EDGAR'. It sounds like a deep, guttural masculine voice. The odd thing about this EVP is that I wasn't trying to contact a spirit at that time. I was only walking from one haunted location to another. I decided to leave the tape recorder on. I was astonished to find out that I finally got an EVP. I had tried several times, at various locations, but I was never successful in getting one.

EVP stands for (Electric Voice Phenomenon); this usually is a disembodied voice that is recorded at a haunted location. Many ghost hunters try to communicate with spirits by asking them several questions, hoping they will answer and get an EVP. The

EVP is usually not heard at the time of questioning. It is not until the voice recorder is played back, that the EVP is heard. Usually it's only a few words, hardly ever a complete sentence.

The Stanley Hotel is a beautiful white and red Georgian style structure built in the Southern hilltop above Estes Park village. F.O. Stanley was the creator of the Stanley Steam Engine. This was a steam powered horseless carriage. He built this hotel in the early 1900's. It opened in 1909.

The hotel is known as the most haunted location in Colorado. This hotel is very active with spirits. The great Steinway piano plays by itself, phantom children have been heard running up and down the hallways, F. O. Stanley's ghost has been seen wandering around the first floor and Lord Dunraven, a wealthy scoundrel and ladies man has been seen on the forth floor.

Stephen King was inspired to write the "Shining" when he stayed with his wife at this hotel in 1972. King stayed in Room 217. He never did reveal if he had any experiences in the room, but it is known to be haunted. In 1995, the Shining TV mini-series was filmed at the Stanley Hotel. One of the crewmembers heard whispering voices behind her in the empty lobby when she was arranging furniture.

An incident happened in Room 217 in the early years of the hotel, when the rooms were still heated by gas lamps. A maid entered the room to light a lamp. She turned on the gas and then discovered she had no matches. She left the room to go get some, not realizing that the gas lamp valve was open. When she came back and lit a match, the accumulated gas exploded. She flew through the floor and landed in the dining room below. She broke both legs and suffered other injuries; however she did survive this awful accident. F.O. Stanley was very generous and covered all her medical expenses. He gave her a raise and promotion when she finally returned to work. She was a very loyal and dedicated worker and continued her employment for many years after the accident.

It is rumored that her ghost haunts Room 217. Guests have reported leaving their luggage on the bed and leaving their room, to go to dinner. Upon returning, their clothes were unpacked and neatly put away.

Another guest said he left his room a mess with clothes everywhere, and then he went to sleep. When he woke up he noticed that his clothes were folded and placed in the drawers. His shoes were neatly lined up near the doorway. He thought someone came in while he was sleeping. A hotel staff member told him there were no maids working at that time, and they would never enter a room while someone was sleeping.

The fourth floor also has a lot of paranormal activity. This area is haunted by ghostly children and Lord Dunraven.
The Stanley Hotel catered to the very elite society when it first opened. The guests would arrive with nannies to care for their children. The children stayed with the nannies on the fourth floor. They were not allowed to run throughout the hotel.

Several guests have reported hearing children running up and down the fourth floor hallways in the middle of the night, even when there is no-one staying in the rooms at the time. An apparition of a little girl has been sighted running in the hallway then disappearing.

Lord Dunraven has also been spotted on the fourth floor near Room 418. If someone enters the room, they feel like they have been grabbed. Some people reported smelling the scent of cigar smoke in the corner of the Billiards Room. Lord Dunraven spent a lot of time on the fourth floor charming the nannies. His ghost has been seen peering out of Room 407. He is dressed in clothing of the late 19th Century.

Lord Dunraven was a foreigner who took advantage of the law that stated only American citizens could purchase land. F. O. Stanley purchased the land for the Stanley Hotel from Lord Dunraven. A guest reported seeing a man standing at the foot of her bed, smoking a cigar. She saw a portrait of Lord Dunraven downstairs in the main lobby and identified this as the same man.

The ghost of F.O. Stanley has been seen at the registration desk and at the bar. His wife Flora, also has been known to make her ghostly presence known. On the first floor, in the Music Room is a Steinway piano. F.O. Stanley gave this to his wife as a present. The piano has been heard playing throughout the hotel at various hours. As soon as someone enters the room, the piano stops. Guests and workers claim that they have seen a shadowy presence seated at the keyboard and the keys were moving by themselves.

One of the main hot spots of spiritual energy is the stairwell going up to the second and third floors. Many psychics and paranormal investigators claim there is a vortex of energy located here. I took many pictures of this area. Although I didn't get any paranormal activity in my photographs, I did feel a little creepy in some of the hallways.

I wonder whose voice it is on the EVP that I recorded? Could it be F. O. Stanley still overseeing his beautiful hotel making sure everyone is doing their jobs and the guests are being taken care of or could it be Lord Dunraven trying to get my attention? Could he still be scheming and bugging the ladies that come to the hotel? This was definitely one intriguing hotel that I will return to and hopefully find some answers.

ARIZONA

WILLIAMS
2007-2008

THE RED GARTER BED AND BAKERY

In the 1800's, the American fur trade extended into Arizona by trappers known as "Mountain Men". One of the most experienced was William Shirley Williams. He enjoyed retreating to the area that was later named after him. Land speculators waiting for construction of a new railroad made claims to various neighborhoods, which are now, part of Williams. The first post office in Williams was established in 1881.

In September 1882, the railroad known as the Santa Fe line was established. The town of Williams became the center for railroad, ranching and lumber industries. Trips to the Grand Canyon by stagecoach were the start of the tourism industry.

By the turn of the century, Williams had a reputation as a rough and rowdy frontier town. It had saloons, brothels, gambling houses and opium dens. This attracted railroad workers, Chinese laborers, loggers, and cowboys. Many of these businesses were restricted by ordinance to a street called Railroad Avenue. These Underground businesses were known as "Saloon Row".

In 1901, a huge fire swept through the town burning 36 business buildings, 2 hotels, and 10 homes in less then an hour. In a week the town was rebuilt and the fire district was formed. Later that year in September, the Santa Fe Railway line was completed. The railroad was 60 miles long. This established Williams as the

"Gateway to the Grand Canyon". This railroad was shut down for 20 years due to the competition of automobiles. It was re-opened in 1989. Today it now carries 200,000 visitors a year.

In 1926, US Highway 66 was established through Williams. This was one of the main streets of America. It became the last "Route 66" town to be bypassed by Interstate 40 in 1984. The downtown business district was placed on the National Register of Historic Places.

Williams is a quaint little town with everything a tourist can need. Saloons, bordellos (Red Garter Bed & Bakery), and shops have been brought back to life by local merchants in order to bring business back into town.

The steam engine departs daily from the Grand Canyon Railway & Resort at the Williams Depot in route to the Grand Canyon. There are many motels and dozens of restaurants to choose from. Williams is very beautiful and scenic. This area has the largest population of Ponderosa pine trees in the world. It hovers at an elevation of 6,700 feet above sea level.

The Red Garter Bed & Bakery is located on 137 W Railroad Avenue, this street is commonly known as "Saloon Row", which is in the business district. It is listed on the National Register of Historic Places for its Victorian Romanesque architecture. It is a beautifully restored two-story brick building.

In 1897, it was originally built as a saloon and bordello by August Tetzaff. The business flourished until 1940. Then it became a Chinese restaurant, opium den, general store, and a boarding house. During 1901 until the late 1930's, the saloon had a two-story out-house located in the backyard. This outhouse was built after the town's huge fire. It was torn down many years ago after indoor plumbing was installed. Now there is a small apartment building there. This is currently where the tour guide resides.

In the seventies, John Holst purchased the old bordello. He restored the historical building, re-creating the atmosphere of the 1890's. The three main rooms have been remolded and each has a unique history. The Parlor Room is where anxious men raced up and down the hallway waiting their turn to see the ladies. The Madam's Room was for the lady in charge of the prostitutes. The Honeymoon Suite is where the top of the line girls would lean out the front windows to wave customers in for a good time. This room is in the front of the building overlooking Railroad Ave.

The legend states a tragic murder was committed on the steps leading up to the rooms on the second floor. A prostitute stabbed one of her clients in the back, causing him to fall down the stairs and through the front door. Then he stumbled onto the street and died.

There have been several accounts of ghostly activity reported throughout the building. The most prominent activity is on the stairs. There are nightlights that line the stairway and flash on when motion detectors are triggered by movement. Sometimes for no apparent reason they flicker on and off as though someone were moving up the steps. The lights have been replaced several times and this eerie phenomenon still occurs.

A picture was taken in the Red Garter Saloon during the Depression. This was downstairs where the bakery is now located. It is a picture of a former owner, Longino Mora, with his wife and child. In the background is a mysterious woman standing behind the counter. She looks Mexican and has long dark hair. She is dressed in a white flowing gown. She is standing in front of a mirror, but it does not reflect her image. This woman is known to be called "Eve." She is usually seen in Room #1, the Honeymoon Suite, also known as the "Best Gals Room." She has been known to wake up guests by pushing slightly down on their mattresses and leave kisses on the arms of unsuspecting visitors. When they wake up no one is there. Some employees have seen the ghost of Eve going from room to room. A few guests have reported "seeing Eve in their dreams". Some people feel that someone has entered their room during the middle of the night. Some guests have reported seeing a Hispanic, dark- haired woman holding a pillbox very tightly. She had a distraught, sad look on her face. She is pacing the floor near the foot of the bed and then she vanishes. Guests have reported hearing doors slamming and footsteps in the hall and on the staircase. The owner has heard a loud "clunk" on many nights. He said it sounded like a heavy door being firmly shut.

I went on the Williams ghost tour October 23, 2007. The tour started in a bookstore, a few buildings down from the Red Garter Bed and Bakery. Our tour guide is a paranormal investigator and was very informative. She took us to several haunted locations in Williams, including a bar, hotel, the train depot, some stores, and finally the Red Garter Bed and Bakery.

There were two women on the ghost tour that were also professional ghost-hunters. They were staying upstairs in Room#1 and offered the group the chance to visit the room if everyone agreed. Everyone was very happy to get a glimpse of the haunted room. We had to climb the steep steps in order to get to our destination. Then we walked around and took photographs inside the haunted room. I didn't see or feel anything unusual. I did however; feel a little strange when I was climbing the narrow staircase upstairs and then when I was walking downstairs.

After everyone exited the building, I snapped a bunch of pictures of the staircase. When the film was developed, the photo contained several streaks of light on the stairs. It seemed like there was movement in the photo. One picture looked like a white mist. The next one showed the lights from the staircase flickering. These looked like previous pictures I have taken at other haunted locations. I also captured red streaks of light in alot of the other photos from around town.

I took a picture of an "Etch A Sketch" in a store window. There have been reports of foul language displayed on the toy. No one was is ever in the store when this happens. In the morning, usually the owner discovers the foul language appearing on the screen. The toy is erased and the following day the writing reappears. I took a picture of this and very prominent streaks of red light appear coming out of the "Etch A Sketch" It is unbelievable.

The tour guide took us to a store that has a statue of a life size Indian that has known to come alive at certain times. The owners believe that the spirit of an Indian that lived in that area possesses the statue. When I walked past this figure, I felt like there was a presence surrounding the table where he sat.

Then we walked towards the train depot. It is near an abandoned building that is full of activity. This is where some people have claimed to see a doppelganger in their photos. I snapped a few photos behind the building and got the same light streaks appearing in the photos.

We proceeded to walk through an alleyway that was next to the bookstore where we started the tour. Everyone from the group had EMF detectors and picked up energy fields walking through this alley. The guide told us several people have been killed in this area many years ago. I snapped a bunch of pictures here and the photos revealed red square dots of light coming out of the sides of the buildings. This was strange since there were absolutely no lights in the alleyway. It was completely dark.

Our group returned to the bookstore. I continued my sweep with the EMF detector. In between the stacks of books, the meter was flashing on and off and beeping like crazy. I took some photos of this area. After all the years of photographing haunted locations, these pictures were the most extraordinary that I have ever taken. One appeared to show two red rays of light coming out of the books on the shelf. Another showed what appeared to be white fuzzy little dots concentrated together. It looked like white static from a television when there is no broadcast. I have never seen anything like that before. The guide told us a young girl was murdered in this very spot where I took these photos. It was a very sad and tragic death and the tour guide didn't even want to enter that area. She said that it upset her so much it was overwhelming.

This was a very exciting tour. It was very informative and I experienced a lot of paranormal activity. I felt a little creepy in certain areas. The whole town of Williams felt haunted, especially since I was walking around in the dark and it was very cold that night. I would like to return to this town and continue with some further investigation.

During the writing of this, I returned to Williams, on September 6th, 2008. My friend and I arrived in town about 11:45pm. Then we went out after midnight to take some pictures. As soon as we pulled into Williams, a black cat crossed our path. Then when I was taking pictures of a location on 3rd Avenue, another black, stray cat followed us everywhere. This was spooky because this is where a phantom cat has been seen climbing the steps of the apartment building that used to be a Masonic Temple. I tried photographing this cat but it was moving very quickly. One picture reveals a vortex right in front of the cat, the other I thought was very cool. It's a photo of the black cat casting two shadows. They are on both sides of the cat.

I proceeded to take pictures of the barn near the Williams depot, the Grand Canyon Hotel, the Sultana Bar, and Rods Steakhouse. These locations are all reported to be haunted. Then I went to the Red Garter Bed and Bakery. I took pictures of the side of the building and inside on the steps. Once again, I got what appeared to be small streaks of light indicating movement on the staircase.

Then I walked over to the alleyway next to the Red Garter. This alley is a ruin of a building that was burned down in 1901.This is where I got a lot of paranormal photos the year before. This seems to be where the highest levels of activity are concentrated. My EMF detector was pegged to the maximum number. It was beeping and flashing on and off. I've never seen a reading so high. My friend had dowsing rods, and they were crossing each other where I was standing. All of a sudden it was freezing. The base reading that night was 56degrees. The temperature in the spot where I was standing fluctuated drastically. It went down to 25 degrees and then down into the negative digits. I tried to use my EVP recorder but the batteries went dead. I had just checked the battery before we left and it was fully charged. Then my camera wouldn't work. The battery was draining very rapidly. I also had a digital camera so my friend took a photo of me at this spot to see if there was anything surrounding me or that area. At that point, a man walked around the corner and startled us. He introduced himself as the new tour guide of the ghost tour. We told him that we were here a year ago and went on the tour. We returned to see if we could capture anything else on film. He said the past few days there have been a lot of strange things going on in this area and around town. This just validated the things that we were experiencing that night.

The next morning, we took a stroll through town. I found the store where the haunted Indian statue sits at the table. It is called the Turquoise Teepee. Unfortunately, the store was closed, so I tried to take a picture through the window. Then I found the store where the haunted Etch A Sketch was located. I couldn't find it the night before because the store is no longer there. It must have gone out of business. There is a hair salon in its place. Right next to the salon is a store called Fabrics and Wooden Things. This store has a sign in the window that states that this is a certified haunted building. The Ghost Hunters International has conducted an investigation and has gathered several pieces of evidence validating this claim. We walked inside and I was automatically drawn to the front of the store. I could feel a strong presence. I continued to walk towards the back of the building. There was another separate room and when I walked in, the presence got stronger and it felt like someone was in the room with me watching my every move. The air became thick and hard to breathe. We made our purchases, chatted with the old man who worked there, and then left Williams that day. Once again, the trip was well worth it. I could feel the paranormal activity in the air and experienced many strange things while visiting the haunted town of gunslingers and cowboys.

Red Garter Bed & Bakery
Williams, AZ. 10/2007
(Strange vortexes appear on staircase)

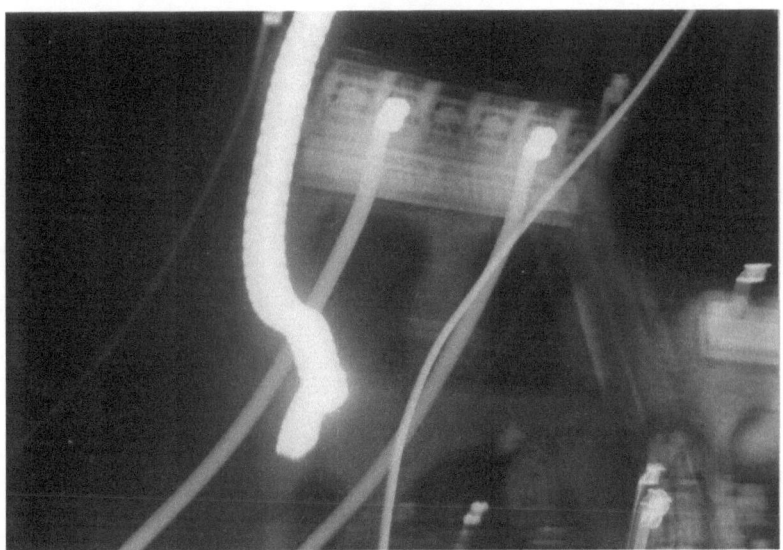

Red Garter Bed & Bakery
Williams, Az. 10/2007
(Vortexes in front of the building)

Red Garter Bed & Bakery
Williams, AZ. 10/2007
(Vortexes appearing in abandoned alleyway next to the
Red Garter – there is no light source)

Red Garter Bed & Bakery
Williams, AZ. 10/2007
(Vortexes appearing in abandon alleyway next to the
Red Garter – there is no light source)

Red Garter Bed & Bakery
Williams, AZ. 10/2007
(Dot-like vortexes appearing in abandon alleyway next to the
Red Garter – there is no light source)

Bookstore where a girl was murdered (Strange static-like phenomenon)
Williams, AZ. 10/2007

Haunted "Etch a Sketch" in a store window
Williams, AZ. 10/2007

Vortexes appearing near Train Station
Williams, AZ. 10/2007

Vortexes appearing near Train Station
Williams, AZ. 10/2007

Cat with double shadow
Williams, AZ. 9/2008

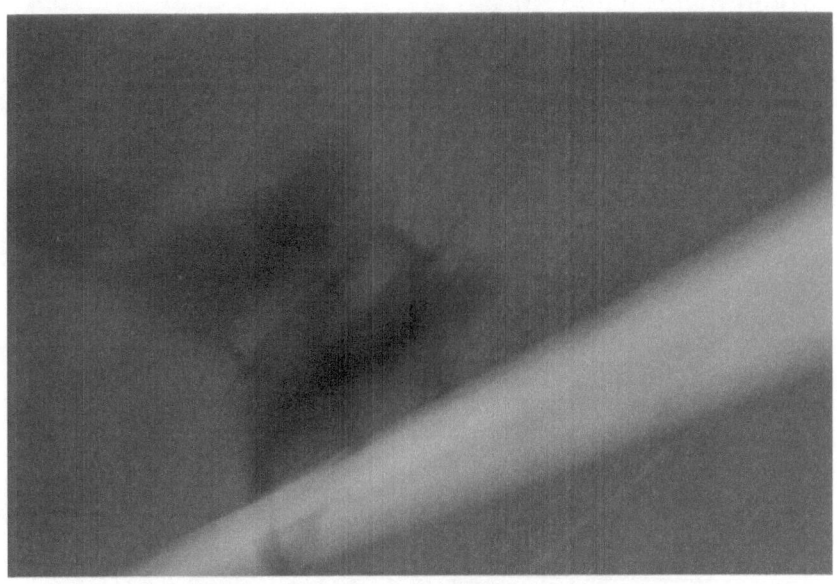

Vortex going through cat
Williams, AZ. 9/2008

HISTORIC GRAND CANYON HOTEL

The Grand Canyon Hotel is a small, historic two story hotel in Williams, Arizona. It was built in 1891, and is a European style building. It has twenty five rooms. It is seasonal and is only open from March 15th to December 1st. This was one of the many haunted locations that we stopped by on the ghost tour in 2007.

The upstairs hallway and a few rooms are reported to be haunted. A man that was attending our tour was staying in one of the haunted rooms. He wanted to show us the haunted room, but the managers didn't want a group of people wandering around the hotel. I guess they didn't want us to disturb the other guests staying there that night. I tried doing some research to find out why this place is haunted, but I wasn't able to find anything.

I took a couple of pictures of the outside of this building. A very bright, white vortex appeared near the upstairs window of the room that is haunted.

Grand Canyon Hotel
Williams, AZ. 10/2007
(Vortex appeared in front of the Grand Canyon Hotel)

CANYON CLUB

One of the last stops on the ghost tour was in front of a local bar named The Canyon Club. It has been around for many years. The bar is located next to the vacant alleyway and the Red Garter Bed & Bakery.

I have gotten the highest concentration of energy with my EMF detector when I walked through this alleyway as well as many paranormal photos.

I took a picture of the side of this building. There are strange white streaks of light coming from the alleyway shooting towards the bar. No one knows who haunts this building. There have been several reports claiming that objects have been moved around the bar area and voices have been heard late at night.

Could these vortexes be a portal into another dimension? Or could it be the ghosts that haunt the Red Garter Bed & Bakery walking over to this bar? Could this be the ladies of the night looking for some business?

Canyon Club
Williams, AZ. 10/2007
(Vortexes shooting towards the bar from the abandon alleyway)

FLAGSTAFF
2007 & 2008

THE MUSEUM CLUB (THE ZOO)

In 1931, Dean Eldredge purchased a piece of federal land, three miles west of Flagstaff, Arizona on Route 66. He hired unemployed Lumberjacks to cut trees, haul them to his property and build what he called "the biggest log cabin in Arizona." He filled it with a lifetime collection of stuffed animals, six-legged sheep, Winchester rifles, Indian artifacts, two-headed calves, and more than 30,000 other items.

He decided to make this building a museum, taxidermist shop, and a trading post. He operated this building for five years. The locals nicknamed the museum the "The Zoo." The name stuck with this building to this day. Eldredge passed away from cancer and most of his collection was sold. In 1936, a saddle maker named Doc Williams purchased the building. He opened a nightclub that was very successful.

Over the years, the building had several owners. It survived as a nightclub, recording studio, and a roadhouse.

In 1963, Don Scott, a steel guitarist bought the club and moved with his wife Thorna to Flagstaff. He turned the club into a country music dance hall. He booked Waylon Jennings and Willie Nelson. Scott, also known as "Pappy", had many contacts in the music industry and he put the club "on the map" in the Western swing circuit. Many new country-recording acts would come from Nashville to Las Vegas, and would be booked to play at the Museum Club.

One time, country singer Barbara Mandrel, showed up at the club, she picked up a guitar and played onstage to the eager crowd. It was a very exciting time for the owners as well as the audience.

Don and Thorna Scott ran the country club until 1973. They lived in the upstairs apartment. One late night, Thorna headed up the stairs to retire for the evening. She suddenly tripped and fell from the top of the stairs. She broke her neck and lapsed into a coma. A few weeks later she passed away and left behind her very depressed and lonely husband, Don. In 1975, Don couldn't take the loneliness anymore and shot himself in front of the fireplace.

The building sat vacant for three years until 1978, when Martin and Stacie Zanzucchi bought the building and began extensive restorations. Today the "Zoo", is still a popular roadhouse bar that has Western music and dancing.

The club is rumored to be haunted by the previous owners Don and Thorna Scott. Creaks have been heard upstairs in the apartment where they once lived. Chairs have been seen rocking on their own, and fires have been started when no one is around. An apparition of Thorna has been seen on the back stairway and in one of the dark booths near the dance floor. She disappears when someone approaches her. One man who lived upstairs claimed to have been pinned down by a friendly female ghost. She then suddenly disappeared.

One bartender said that when she started her shift the bar shelves were disarrayed. She was shocked to see this, because she had worked the night before and had straightened everything up. There was no one else working that night or the next afternoon before she came in.

Many people have taken pictures and videos of the club and have reported ghostly images appearing on film. Lights flicker on and off in the building when it is closed and no one is there.

I have gone to this bar several times and photographed the outside of this building. An orb appeared floating in the air in one of the pictures. Over Labor Day weekend, I went there on a Saturday night with a couple of friends. I was finally able to photograph the inside of the building. I loved the beautiful woodwork structure. There are still several stuffed animals and antlers hanging from the walls. Each table is carved from wood in a unique shape. There is a huge dance floor with a very small stage.

When I first walked inside, I went past the fireplace and then walked to the left side of the building. The atmosphere felt a little strange and I could sense a presence there. It didn't feel threatening, just like someone was watching me and perhaps over seeing the activity in the club.

Could it be Don and Thorna still haunting this club? They loved the music and the business so much that they don't want to be away from it. They may be clinging on to this location because this is where they were the happiest, or they may not know that they have passed on to another dimension. They are still running their business from the afterlife.

The Museum Club (The Zoo)
Flagstaff, AZ. 9/2007
(Multiple orbs were surrounding the side of the building)

HOTEL MONTE VISTA
9/03/08 & 2/15/09

On Labor Day weekend, I took a road trip with a couple of friends to Flagstaff, Arizona. We stopped for a drink at the haunted Hotel Monte Vista. We walked downstairs to the bar. As I was passing through the narrow corridor I felt a little uneasy. I could sense a presence in the hallway. It felt like something was standing behind me. I snapped a picture and a large orb appeared in the hallway exactly where I thought I felt something. I also came back to the hotel many hours later to photograph the building at night. The sky was very calm and clear with just a little chill in the air. The town was very busy and there were a lot of people walking around.

I took a couple of pictures of the outside of the hotel with my digital camera. I was astonished when I saw the results. There were multi-colored vortexes coming from the building. It looked like the vortexes are shooting downwards. There is so much paranormal activity going on in the photo, it's amazing. This is the same kind of intense photographs that I took when I was in Salem, Massachusetts and Gettysburg, Pennsylvania.

When I took these pictures, my two close friends were with me. They couldn't believe what the photos revealed either. When you look at the digital camera screen, numerous anomalies appear that you cannot see with the naked eye.

In the 1920's the citizens of Flagstaff agreed they needed a first class hotel to keep the tourists in the area. They wanted the out of towners to spend their money to help the local economy thrive.

In 1924, an astronomer headed up a local fundraiser that established a municipal bond to build the hotel. Novelist Zane Gray put up the remainder of the money needed to build this hotel. It is an impressive fourteen-story structure of brick, steel, and concrete. It was built on a corner, in the heart of town.

The hotel was originally called the "Community Hotel." In 1927, a contest was held in order to rename it. A 12-year-old girl won. She named the hotel Monte Vista, which means "Mountain View" in Spanish. It was the first full service hotel in Arizona.

Many Hollywood stars have stayed at this hotel during the making of some of their films. A lot of movies were filmed in the Flagstaff and Sedona areas. Some of the rooms are named after the most famous actors that have stayed there. The most famous guests were Humphrey Bogart, Bing Crosby, Debbie Reynolds, Michael J. Fox, Jane Russell, Gary Cooper, John Wayne, Spencer Tracey, Clark Gable, Carole Lombard, Bob Hope, Zane Grey, and Esther Williams.

In the 1960's, the hotel was sold to a private individual. In 1986, the restoration process began. It has been returned to its original style and luster. Today, it is on the National Register of Historic Places.

There are several ghosts that seem to remain there on different floors.

Room 402; is called the John Wayne Suite. The actor had a ghostly experience when he was staying here filming a movie in the late 1950's. He walked into the sitting room area of the suite and encountered a friendly spirit standing near a table. As he approached the apparition, it disappeared.

On the third floor, one of the guests spotted a moving orb. She grabbed her digital camera and followed it down the hall. It stopped in front of a door, where there was a man standing there. He was going through the motions of unlocking a door. However, he did not open it, he walked right through it. She couldn't believe her eyes. She said the ghost-resembled actor Alan Ladd. When she looked over at the room number – 309, she was shocked to see this was called the Alan Ladd Room. Was this perhaps the ghost of the late actor?

Many people staying in Room 306 claimed to have felt a presence. They feel like they are being watched. There is a rumor that two prostitutes were murdered in that room, and their bodies were thrown out of the window.

Room 305, is nicknamed the "Rocking Chair Room". Each time someone enters the room, the chair ends up in a different spot. Regardless of where the chair winds up, the chair would be facing toward the window. Some guests have reported seeing a female spirit sitting in the chair at night.

The second floor is also quite active. Room 210, The Zane Grey Suite, is also nicknamed the "Phantom Bellboy Room". There have been many reports of guests hearing a phantom bellboy knocking on the door. In a muffled voice, he says "Room Service"! When the guests open the door there is no one there.

In Room 216, the phone rings in the middle of the night. When it is answered there is no one on the line, only "dead air" can be heard.

Room 220 is the last room on the left, at the end of the second floor hallway. Guests staying here experienced an overwhelming feeling of sadness. A long-term boarder stayed in this room in the 1980's. He stayed in the room isolated from the outside world. He was very strange and had eccentric habits. One of the most extreme was that he would hang raw meat from the chandelier in his room. His ghost has been nicknamed "The Meatman". When the man passed away, he went unmissed due to his hermit like behavior. His body lay decomposing for three days before he was discovered. A maintenance man said he was doing repairs in this room when he had an eerie experience. He claims that when he left the room he turned off the light, and locked the door. He returned five minutes later to find the light on, the bedding stripped and the TV blaring full blast.

In room 222, one of the bartenders claimed to have seen and old man. He looked like he was in his 70's with gray hair and a white shirt.

The lowest level of the building also has had some strange occurrences. This is where there is a bar and several tables. Bands play here on the weekends and there is a small dance floor. Bar stools have been seen sliding across the floor on their own. The employees have heard disembodied voices, and TV channels change on their own without anyone using the remote. It is believed the ghost of a bank robber haunts this area. The thief was having a drink with his partners before he expired on the premises. He was shot and killed by a security guard.

This is the hallway where I photographed an orb. It was a long dark corridor leading to the bar. It is possibly the energy left over from the bank robber. This is the area of the building that I felt was most active, at least while I was there.

The last area of the hotel that is haunted is the basement. What has happened down there is unknown. Night auditors have heard a baby crying late at night.

I wasn't able to get to the second or third floor that night, but I want to go back and stay there sometime. Since there has been so much ghostly activity reported, there's no wonder I was able to get such extraordinary photos. I seemed to capture all the energy of the ghosts together in one photo.

I returned to the hotel 6 months later. My friends and I checked into Room 305, at the Hotel Monte Vista. This is also called The Bon Jovi Room. He stayed in that room on his way to a performance in Phoenix, Arizona many years ago. Each room in the hotel has a different color scheme and is named after someone famous who has previously stayed in that room. Room 305 is the most active room for paranormal activity in this hotel. It is also know as "The Rocking Chair Room." An apparition of an old woman has been seen sitting in the chair looking out the window.

We arrived around 5:00pm. This was Presidents Day Weekend and it was also Valentines Day, so every room in the hotel was booked. It was very busy and noisy. There were a lot of people in the hallways, café, and bar. We could hear the train coming through the town blowing the horn every hour.

I took a base reading with my EMF detector (Electronic Magnetic Frequency) which read 1.0 for most of the room. The temperature was 65 degrees inside and outside was 40 degrees. The low for that night was 11 degrees.

Around 10:30pm, I went around the room with my EMF meter and got a 2.0 reading near the bed directly in front of the Rocking Chair. Then I took a reading in front of the heater which pegged to the highest number which was 5.0. I just assumed it was so high because of the electrical heating unit. A few seconds later, I took another reading in both areas. There weren't any readings near the bed or the heater. If the high reading was coming from the heater then it would consistently stay at 5.0, but it didn't, it was 0.0. It was as if something was there then it moved. This indicates paranormal activity.

Then I got out my EVP meter (Electronic Voice Phenomenon). I asked some questions addressing the old woman. I asked if there was a presence in the room with me. Just at that moment, the door opened and closed lightly. It was as if someone was there and then walked out of the room.

Then I set the recorder on the desk and left the room. I did this twice that night. When I reviewed the recordings later on that evening I heard sounds on the tape. I could hear a loud thud, and then creaking on the floor. Then I heard footsteps like someone was walking around in the room but no-one was there at this time.

Around 10:30pm, I took my camera and went outside. I looked up at the window of the room that we were staying in. The lights were flickering on and off. I took four photos of the window with my digital camera. When the pictures were developed, the first two were normal but the third picture was totally black. A few seconds later I took a fourth photo. Red streaks of light appeared underneath the window. I have taken photos of this hotel previously and have gotten similar results.

Around 12:15am, I was back inside the room. I kept looking over at the rocking chair. I felt like there was a presence in the room. I grabbed my camera and took a few photos in the dark. One orb appeared directly above the chair. The second photo showed an orb moving towards the corner of the room. In the third photo the orb appeared moving towards the bed where I got the high EMF reading.

I also walked around the room with dowsing rods. The rods crossed over near the bed where I took a high EMF reading earlier and near the door that opened up on its own. When the rods cross over each other it usually indicates there is a high energy field in that area. Ghost hunters believe this energy is due to paranormal activity. This is also what I believe. It seems too coincidental that both areas omit high energy regardless of what equipment is used. Both the EMF meter and the dowsing rods validate that there was some spiritual energy there at the time the door opened and the orbs appeared. Also the sounds on the tape may indicate something or someone was in the room when we left. The photos to me are the most compelling evidence that there was something paranormal in the room with us that night.

Could it be the spirit of the old lady? If it was, she seems harmless and a non-threatening entity. I told her out loud we were here just to sleep and not bother her, and if she wanted to interact with us it was ok by us. I feel she made her presence known and then left us alone. She may just be a spirit who is choosing to stay on earth and not pass on to another plane due to her own personal reasons. Whatever the reason, I do believe this was a haunted room and I was very excited and satisfied staying there. I would like to come back to this hotel and stay in another haunted room and she if I can experience and document more paranormal activity.

Hotel Monte Vista
Flagstaff, AZ. 2/2009
"The Rocking Chair Room"– (An orb appears above the chair)

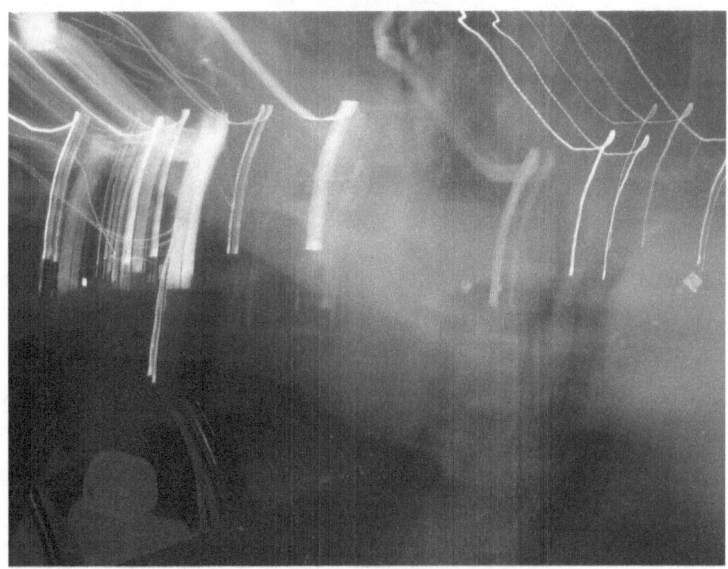

Outside the Hotel Monte Vista
Flagstaff, AZ. 2/2009
(Vortexes above the sidewalk-near parked cars)

The front of the Hotel Monte Vista
Flagstaff, AZ. 2/2009
(Colorful vortexes shooting from the Hotel)

WEATHERFORD HOTEL

My friends and I walked down a block from the Monte Vista to the Weatherford Hotel. I took photos of this building at night and also got some amazing results. Once again, I captured multi-colored vortexes with my digital camera. They seemed to be coming from the outside of the building. I was so happy, because I took a lot of other pictures of haunted locations throughout Flagstaff but I didn't get anything. I have visited Flagstaff many times and each time I took photos but I never saw any paranormal activity in them until tonight. I guess I was at the right place at the right time.

The hotel felt creepy as I walked up the stairs to the balcony. The hallways were dimly lit and the stairs creaked. Upstairs is the haunted ballroom and bar. We got our drinks and sat outside on the balcony. As we were sitting there, it started to drizzle. The hotel was bustling with activity. It was a perfect night to capture paranormal activity.

The Weatherford Hotel was built in 1898. The hotel was originally a much smaller building. There was a general store on the first floor and the Weatherford family lived upstairs.

In 1900, they added a three-story addition to the hotel. One of the outstanding features included a new ballroom surrounded by a three- sided balcony. The bar within the ballroom is an elaborately carved counter imported from the Palace Hotel Saloon in Tombstone, Arizona.

There was a fire in 1929 that damaged the balcony and the cupola. Recently, this area has been renovated to its original structure. At one time, this was one of the most distinguished hotels in Flagstaff. Publisher William Randolph Hearst, artist Thomas Moran and writer Zane Grey stayed here. Zane wrote one of his novels while staying at the Weatherford Hotel. The ballroom was named after him.

The Weatherford has been a theater, billiard hall, radio-station, and several restaurants since it opened. The historical preservation efforts have won several awards especially the work on the balcony and the ballroom.

Upstairs in the ballroom, several employees have experienced ghostly activity. They have seen drinks sliding down the length of the bar. A ghostly figure of a girl has been seen floating across the room early in the morning. There have also been reports of employees hearing their names called in the third floor hallway. Then there is a sensation that someone is standing behind them looking over his or her shoulders, when they turn around, no-one is there.

Room 54 is probably the most haunted. A newlywed couple rented this room a long time ago. The couple began arguing. The argument became so heated and intense that a murder was committed. This room is now a storage closet. Many guests have reported seeing a man and a woman enter this room. A former employee had a frightening experience. She woke in the middle of the night and saw a couple sitting on the edge of her bed. They were dressed in their wedding attire as if they were just married. They got up and walked through the door.

The basement is another part of the hotel that is haunted. Kitchen employees often hear someone walking up and down the basement steps. One of the staff's members dog was afraid to cross a certain area of the basement, no matter how much he was coaxed. He sensed something there that he could not see. A man named Noah, was a bootlegger during the Prohibition era. Legend states that he was murdered and robbed by another bootlegger in the dark catacombs of the basement. His ghost probably still lingers there.

Weatherford Hotel
Flagstaff, AZ. 9/2008
(Multi-colored vortexes appear outside the building)

CALIFORNIA

SAN DIEGO
2008

WILLIAM HEATH DAVIS HOUSE

(GASLAMP QUARTER DISTRICT)

William Heath Davis tried to develop modern San Diego, Ca. He purchased 8–10 pre- framed "salt box" family homes. They were shipped from Maine by a ship called "The Cybell." They were originally set up on his land where the historic "Star of India" ship is currently docked in San Diego, Ca.

The William Heath Davis home was set up on the corner of State and Market streets. William rented this house to military officers. He set up another house for his personal residence. William actually never lived in the William Heath Davis House.

In 1867, Alonzo E Horton and his wife bought the house. They also purchased the land surrounding Davis' property. Alonzo planned to build a new town near the water. He was very successful in marketing and convinced many people to move to San Diego from all over the country. Alonzo is credited with being the founder of San Diego. Most of the historic buildings in the Gas Lamp District are the results of Alonzo's investments to promote the new town. Eventually, Horton made a huge profit and moved into a mansion, leaving the small house behind.

For years, the house had several owners. In 1873, the house was purchased by Anna Shepard. She had the house moved to the corner of "11ᵗʰ" and "K" streets. She opened it as a county hospital. A total of 19 sick people resided there at one time. Most people were treated for tuberculosis and various injuries.

In the early 1900's, the house was purchased by the Lohmans. They loved the house and wanted to protect its historical value. They rented a room in the attic to a man who was a German Spy during WWI.

They met George Deyo, whom they liked very much. They offered him a deal. The Lohmans said when they die; he may remain living in the house, rent free, as long as he promised not to change anything in the house. He moved in and kept his promise. Many years later, George took in a retired couple, named the Lanzas and offered them the same deal. They also agreed not to change anything in the house. This is why there wasn't any electricity in the house for many years. The only major modification was in 1911, when indoor plumbing was installed.

In 1984, the house was moved to its present location, on the corner of 4ᵗʰ and Island Ave. The city of San Diego now owned this house. The William Heath Davis house was refurbished, electricity was installed, and it was opened as a museum.

This house is the oldest wooden structure standing in San Diego. Each room in the museum is decorated to represent a different period in the life of this historic home.

There has been a lot of ghostly activity reported in the house throughout its many years of operation.

In 1977, the occupants of the house reported seeing lights going on and off by themselves. A local newspaper featured an article on this occurrence. The strange thing about this is that there wasn't any electricity in the house until 1984. The lights were either gas or coal oil lamp flames; which requires a match to light. The house still has reports of lights going on and off. This usually occurs when there isn't anyone in the house. Every night all the lights are turned off before the security alarm is set. Many times, the following morning, a light is found turned on in the back room of the house.

Gold braided ropes are used to guide the flow of tours from one room to another. These ropes are placed across the doorways after the last tour of the day. On several occasions, the following morning, the staff has discovered that the ropes are laying on the floor as if someone took them off their hooks.

An apparition of a Victorian woman has been seen near the top of the stairs, leading to the second floor. She is wearing a long skirt with petticoats and high-button shoes. Most of the time, she is only seen from the waist down. Several people from the ghost tour, stated that they had seen a woman in full costume, invite them to come upstairs. When they told the tour guide, he was surprised. He said there were no guides fitting that description working that day and no one was upstairs at the time.

On the second floor, sometimes cold spots and a chilling breeze can be felt, even during the summer months.

In the "Hospital Room", there is a medicine chest that always has its lid left open. Upon returning to work the next day, the employees find the lid closed shut. Other items in this room have been moved around during the night. Cold spots have been felt along the west wall, near the door. Some visitors sense an overwhelming presence near the doorway of this room.

The Victorian woman has also been seen near the Childs Room on the second floor. There are many antique items from 1880 in this room.

On the first floor, there is a room on the left side as soon as you walk in, called the Military Room. This was a room that housed military officers at one time. There is furniture and clothing on display that dates back from 1850-1860. The rope barrier has also been known to move in the doorway during the nighttime.

The last haunted area is the dining room. This room is furnished with items from 1886-1900. The dishes and silverware have been moved during the night by an unseen presence.

The night that I went on this tour, I didn't expect to get any paranormal activity appearing in the photos because the streets of San Diego were very noisy and busy. I usually don't get anything paranormal under these conditions.

It was a clear, warm night. There was no rain, wind, or extreme heat or cold. It was a perfect evening.

Before the tour started, a number of people congregated outside, in front of the William Heath House. There is a little patio, with a few benches and some trees.

I snapped a couple of pictures with my digital camera of the front of the house. I viewed the photos immediately and saw some very prominent streaks of light coming from the right hand side of the house. Just at that moment, something hard struck my right upper arm. It startled me and my arm hurt very badly for at least 10 minutes after the incident. I looked around to see what it could have been that hit me, but it was dark and I couldn't see anything. I thought maybe something fell from a tree, but I wasn't near any at the time. This was scary because it felt like someone punched me in the arm, as if it were trying to get my attention. I automatically thought something wanted to let me know it was there. I thought this was strange because this happened only seconds after I discovered the anomaly in the picture.

The rest of the tour was interesting, but uneventful. Our tour guide took us though the streets of the gas-lamp district. We went past the Horton Hotel, where the ghost of Wyatt Earp has been seen playing cards on the third floor. We also walked past a haunted theatre, Thai restaurant, and steam tunnels that run under the streets of San Diego.

One of our last stops was an office building that was an orphanage at one time. I took several photos of this building. I did get a few orbs in some of the photos. They seem to be appearing near the third floor, where there has been ghostly activity. Office equipment and supplies have been moved around during the night when no-one is there. The employees discover this the following morning. Sounds of children laughing and talking have been heard throughout the building. One employee claimed to have seen an apparition of a little girl running through the hallway.

As I walked through the William Heath House, I took photos of the parlor, the kitchen, the military room and the staircase. We were not allowed to go upstairs, so I didn't get to explore the Children's Room or the Medicine Room. I didn't capture anything on film from the pictures that I took. The only strange experience that I had was outside, which was good enough for me.

I would like to go back someday and take another tour of the entire house, which is only offered in the daytime.

It is hard to determine how many spirits haunt this house. There is an abundance of history about how many people lived in this house. Could it just be the mysterious Victorian woman who roams these hallways, military soldiers, or some other spirit that may inhabit the William Heath House? One thing is for certain, I had a hair- raising experience that I will never forget.

William Heath Davis House
San Diego, CA. 11/2008
(Vortexes on the right side of the house)

William Heath Davis House
San Diego, CA. 11/2008
(Vortexes appeared where I felt something hit my arm)

Gaslamp Quarter District
San Diego, CA. 11/2008
(A large pinkish orb in front of a haunted building)

Old Orphanage
(Gaslamp Quarter District)
San Diego, CA. 11/2008
(A large orb appears near haunted third floor)

THE WHALEY HOUSE

We arrived at Old Town, San Diego about 9:30pm. We walked over to the Whaley House the night before our tour. The tours are only available in the daytime, but I wanted to photograph the grounds and the building in the dark. I usually am able to get a lot more ghostly phenomenon at nighttime. It's easier to see the anomalies in the night photos.

I didn't know that much history about the house at this point. I was uncertain about the haunted hot spots of this house, so I just snapped pictures according to my own instincts. When I felt some kind of presence or eerie feeling in a certain spot I took a picture.

I first walked on the steps and looked through the windows. I was immediately drawn to the courtroom. I took a few photos with my digital camera through the window. When I viewed the picture there appeared to be a filmy light and a big pinkish orb.

Then I walked around the back of the house and took a photo of the upstairs middle window. This is on the second floor. One very big prominent orb appeared. I found out the next day that an apparition of a man, who is thought to be Yankee Jim, has appeared in this very spot. This is also the same staircase that several people claim to have seen a strange man looking out the middle window.

I walked over to the backyard. I shot some pictures of the area where the gallows used to be. Several orbs appeared in the photos where people were hanged.

Then I walked over to the side of the Whaley House. There was a small walkway and I felt an eerie presence there. I took a photo and an orb appeared directly in front of me. The property felt very haunted to me. I could feel a lot of energy concentrated in certain locations.

The next day before the tour, I went to the gift shop next to the Whaley House. The cashier told us that that she used to work inside the Whaley House giving tours for many years until she had a scary experience. She said one night she was alone closing up the rooms. She was walking upstairs and stopped for a second to look around and then she felt a hand brush through her hair very lightly. She screamed and ran out of the building. The woman stated that she had seen shadows and has heard noises throughout the years that she had worked there. This was the first time that something had touched her. She quit her job at the Whaley House the next day. She left San Diego for a few years. The owners begged her to come back to work at the Whaley House. She refused. They were very persistent so she finally compromised and said she would work only in the daytime and only at the gift shop, which is in a different building, The owners were happy because she was very friendly with the visitors and it was good for business. She was a great lady to talk to and filled me in on the history of the house.

It was awesome to talk to someone who actually had a paranormal experience in the Whaley House.

I took the tour of the house during the daytime and finally had a chance to take pictures of the inside of the house. I was drawn to the courtroom, which is located on the first floor. This is where I sensed the most paranormal activity. I took many pictures but nothing unusual came out from the daytime photos. I did feel a little eerie when I was on the staircase walking towards the old theatre. I didn't feel threatened, just like I was being watched and followed.

Thomas Whaley left NYC on 1/01/1849, on a ship named the "Sutton." He arrived in San Francisco 204 days later. This was during the Gold Rush. He set up a store selling hardware and woodwork with his business partner George Wardle.

In May 1851, an arson- set fire destroyed his buildings. He relocated to Old Town, San Diego. There he set up various businesses and made enough money to return to NYC to marry Anna Eloise DeLaunary.

Upon returning to San Diego, he had various general store business partnerships, most of which lasted less then a year.

In 1855, he purchased the property which the Whaley House was built on. In May of 1856, he built a single-story granary with bricks manufactured in his own brickyard. The adjacent two- story Greek Revival style brick building that was designed by Whaley was finished in 1857. This building was the first, and the finest brick building in Southern California.

In 1857, Whaley established his general store there. The location was too far from the center of town so he relocated his business to a wood-frame building near the Plaza.

Thomas and Anna had a total of six children. One of their sons's died when he was 18 months old.

In 1858, another arson-set fire destroyed Whaley's business so he returned to San Francisco. There he worked as an U.S. commissary storekeeper.

In 1868, a major earthquake hit San Francisco. Whaley decided to move his family back to San Diego. He opened up a General Store with a partner named Philip Crosthwaite. Whaley rented the upstairs western portion of the house to Mr. Thomas Tanner. Tanner transformed the living quarters into San Diego's first commercial theater. Three months later Tanner suddenly died.

In 1869, The County of San Diego rented the theater space and the former granary for use as meeting rooms for the Board of Supervisors and one of San Diego's earliest courthouses.

Since the establishment of Old Town by Alonzo Horton, the seat of government moved there.

Whaley returned to New York in 1873 to settle his father's estate. He was having financial problems so he returned to San Francisco searching for employment. His wife and children remained in San Diego.

The Whaley House was rented out for many years and eventually fell into disrepair.

In 1909, Whaley's oldest son Francis; returned to the old brick house and undertook the restoration of the building. He utilized it as a tourist attraction, promoting its historical significance and entertained visitors with his guitar.

In 1913, Anna died in the house, followed by Francis in 1914. Lillian his sister remained in the house writing memoirs until she passed away in 1953.

In 1956, the house was put up for sale. There were plans to demolish the house and make it into a gas station. Luckily, June and Jim Reading, with a group of local citizens convinced the County of San Diego to buy, restore, and open the home to the public by creating a museum. This was opened in 1960.

The Whaley House was also a ballroom, billiard hall, school, and polling place.

There were some significant events that took place here that have affected Thomas and Anna Whaley while they were living in the house. One was the seizure of the court documents and records in 1871. Many of the local citizens opposed to the courtroom being located in this building. Another tragedy was the suicide of Violet Whaley in 1885. Also there were several hangings that occurred on the property before the house was constructed.

The Whaley House is the number one most haunted house in the United States, according to the travel channel's TV-show "America's Most Haunted."

"Yankee Jim", whose real name is James (aka Santiago) Robinson is known to haunt the Whaley House. In 1852, he was convicted of attempted grand larceny in San Diego. He was hanged on a gallows off the back of a wagon on the property where the house now stands. Thomas Whaley was present at the hanging, but it did not discourage him from buying the property and building a house. Shortly after the Whaley's moved in, they heard heavy footsteps moving around the house. They were described as sounds of heavy boots of a large man. Whaley thought the unexplained noises were made by the ghost of Yankee Jim Robinson.

A visitor experienced the sounds of walking and the windows unlatch and open up. Other visitors experienced encountering the spirit of Thomas Whaley. They have seen an apparition of him in the parlor and on the upper landing. He was dressed in old fashioned clothing from the early 1800's. When someone looked directly at him, his face turned away and then he vanished into thin air.

The spirit of Anna Whaley has also been sighted in the downstairs rooms and garden. She appears as a white, translucent, floating and drifting figure.

Other visitors see or sense the presence of a small woman in the courtroom. She is wearing a long skirt, gold hoop earrings, and a cap on her head. She has dark hair and dark eyes.

Some psychics have come to the house and sensed the presence of a young girl in the dining room. There were rumors that a young girl that was playing in the backyard with one of the Whaley children, accidentally hung herself on a clothing line.

One parapsychologist claimed to have seen an apparition of a spotted dog resembling a fox terrier. It ran into the dining room and disappeared. The Whaley's owned a terrier named Dolly Varden. Could this be the spirit of that dog?

Everyday visitors come from around the world to tour this historic museum. It is currently owned by The County of San Diego. SOHO (Save Our Heritage Organization), has managed the property since 2000. They are a non- profit organization and have been a historic preservation advocate since 1969.

The Whaley House
(Old Town) San Diego, CA. 11/2008
(This is in the backyard. An Orb appeared near the second story window
where Yankee Jim's apparition has been seen looking out)

Side Walkway of the Whaley House (Old Town) San Diego, CA. 11/2008
(Multiple orbs appear here.)

The courtroom in the Whaley House
(Old Town) San Diego, CA. 11/2008
Orbs and Mist

The courtroom in the Whaley House
(Old Town) San Diego, CA. 11/2008
(Pinkish Orbs)

The backyard of the Whaley House
(Old Town) San Diego, CA, 11/2008
(Multiple orbs appear where the gallows where located)

LONG BEACH
2008

THE QUEEN MARY HOTEL

The Queen Mary had a very long and glorious past. The time that this ship has spent at sea is divided into three periods. The Early Years (1936-1939), The War Years (1940-1946), and the Post War Years (1947- to her last voyage in 1967).

The first voyage was in May, 1936. The ship carried thousands of people and 6,124 sacks of mail. The BBC installed microphones and it was broadcast around the world.

The Queen Mary sailed from England to New York in four days, and fifteen hours. It docked at Pier 90 on the Hudson River greeted by a cheering crowd.

The Queen Mary entered many contests for the quest for the "Blue Riband." This distinction would go to the ship that performed the fastest transatlantic crossing. The Queen Mary went 35 miles per hour and held this record for 14 years. It was finally beat in 1952, by the "SS United States," which was a much lighter ship that moved faster.

The first class passengers of the Queen Mary were afforded with every luxury and convenience that they asked for. The chefs were experts and hired from the best restaurants in the world. The crew and staff were trained to cater to everyone's needs.

The dining room was the largest room ever built within a ship. It had the largest floor space and seating capacity.

The Queen Mary was less then 229 ft shorter then the Empire State Building, taller then the Eiffel Tower, and over twice as tall as the Pyramid of Cheops. From the keel to the forward funnel, the ship's height is greater then the Niagara Falls. The recreation space is equivalent to a large football stadium. The engines generate a total of 160,000 horse power. The anchors equal the weight of 20 cars. The ship contains 10 miles of carpeting, 700 clocks, and 600 phones. The interior décor was fashioned out of 56 of the world's finest and rarest woods.

Many famous celebrities have sailed abroad the Queen Mary. Some of them include: Fred Astaire, Greta Garbo, Bob Hope, Elizabeth Taylor, Laurel and Hardy and many more. Some prominent figures include: The Duke and Duchess of Windsor, the Baron and Baroness De Rothschild and the Vanderbilts.

During WWII, the Queen Mary was converted to a troop transport ship. It carried 800,000 troops, passengers, and refugees. It was well-equipped for fending off potential air strikes. It carried various weapons, machine guns, and rocket launchers. Prime Minister Winston Churchill was aboard the ship many times during the War Years.

In October of 1942, the Queen Mary was sailing off the coast of Ireland. It accidentally struck its escort cruiser the HMS Curacao, slicing it in half. Three-hundred and thirty eight sailors died at sea.

In 1947, it was converted back to a passenger ship. Due to more improved and time saving modes of transportation, the number of passengers declined, so the ship was sold.

In 1967, the Queen Mary arrived in Long Beach, California and the captain announced the end of the ships long career at sea. It was permanently docked at Pier J and opened as a tourist attraction. It is listed on the National Register of Historic Places. The ship is now a hotel with 365 restored First class rooms, and has award winning dining. It has 50,000 square ft of exhibition space and offers historical as well as ghost tours.

During the War years, soldiers awaited their orders below deck. They dealt with cramped, stifling, and claustrophobic conditions. Many people died due to these factors. It carried prisoners of war as well as dignitaries. They were separated by social class as well. Maybe some of that energy has been left behind on the Queen Mary.

In the ships heyday, royalty and the working class, the young and the old and people of all nationalities sailed together. However, those who worked in the boiler rooms worked in the dark shaft alleys. They hardly saw the light of day during their long trips. They kept the ship in perfect working order and at full speed so those passengers above deck could relax and enjoy their time on their voyage.

I'm sure there was some resentment from the workers. They probably felt like they had to work so hard while other people could just sit back and enjoy their lives. Maybe this is why the ghosts of the boiler room still haunt the ship and try to scare the current visitors.

There have been numerous accounts of strange phenomenon happening aboard the Queen Mary. Doors that are locked one minute mysteriously become unlocked the next, often triggering alarm lights near the swimming pools. There are sounds of footsteps when no one is there; banging and hammering noises as if someone is working on equipment although there isn't any in that area; the clanking of chains and banging on oil drums, voices and laughter echoing in the darkness. Cold spots, gusts of wind in air tight areas, lights going on and off on their own, objects disappearing or being moved and the sound of glasses clinking in the dining area have all been reported by passengers and employees of the Queen Mary.

One of the most famous ghosts on the ship is John Peddler. In 1966, he was trapped in a water tight mechanical door #13 in the Engine Room. The door closed suddenly, and he was crushed to death. His nickname is "The Shaft Alley Specter." His apparition has been seen many times in this area.

William Eric Stark was another man who died on the ship. He accidentally drank a mixture of tetrachloride and lime juice. He lapsed into a coma and died from the effects of the poison. His apparition has also been seen wandering around the ship.

Many visitors have seen a specter of a man in a white suit below deck. He is in his forties and his suit looks like something from the 1930's. Also a man dressed in blue-gray overalls has been heard and seen in the same area. He has jet-black hair and a long beard. He is possibly a member of the maintenance crew.

Three different spirits have been sighted in the pool area. One is of a little girl that our tour guide has contacted. Two is a young attractive woman in a miniskirt, and three is an old woman seen in a swimming cap and an old fashioned bathing suit from the 1920's or 30's.

A Lady in White has been seen in the main Lounge (which is now the Queen's Salon). She is waltzing and lingers near the piano.

A woman dressed in 1940's clothing has been seen sitting at a table in the Promenade Café,

Two women as well as an Italian fighter pilot have been contacted during séances.

Other areas that have ghostly activity are the kitchen, the morgue, and the first class nursery.

Many psychics believe there are about 600 spirits aboard the Queen Mary. The main center of the paranormal activity is concentrated in the below deck areas. This is where there is the most spiritual energy.

I was so excited to go on the tour of the Queen Mary. I have never been on a ship of this caliber before and I was impressed with the massive size. I couldn't believe my eyes as I approached the ship. As soon as I stepped foot through the doorway on to Deck B I felt an overwhelming presence. There was an immediate white haze throughout the long corridors.

I walked down the long hallway on my way to the ladies room. It felt like someone was watching my every step. I felt a strong presence in the bathroom.

Our tour guide was a young psychic who had been working on the ship for the past three years. She said the night seemed very unusual because it was eerily quiet and we were the only two people on the tour. This is the first time that this has happened since she has worked there. It was a very dark night and it was very misty and foggy outside. The cash register, credit card machine, and various other electronic devices had been acting up on and off all day long. She also mentioned that the power had gone out earlier in the day. All this activity is known to happen in areas that have high paranormal activity.

The tour guide took us to a room and told us a little history of the ship and asked us what we expected to get out of the tour. She explained to us that she could communicate with spirits by chan-neling or we could just walk around and do our own investigation. The choice was ours. We both agreed that we prefer to do our own EVP session, take photographs, temperature readings, and use our EMF detectors and dowsing rods.

The psychic seemed to be a trance medium, which means she could 'channel ' a spirit and allow it's presence to enter into her body and speak directly to us. I felt I didn't want her to do this because I was afraid she may contact the wrong kind of spirit. I was sensing a lot of negative energy in certain areas. The Queen Mary has a long history of violent deaths. I believe you can never be sure of what spirit may try to break through. I didn't want something evil following us home. So we just continued to walk to the most active haunted spots of the ship.

The first area we went to was the Pool Area on Deck C. The psychic told us that this was the most active paranormal hot spot on the ship. She also said there were two vortexes in this room and she was curious if I could figure out where they were. I told her that I could sense spirits nearby, even though I can't see or hear them. I told her the first vortex was near the dressing rooms and the second was near the right hand corner of the pool. The psychic was amazed. She said I was one of the very few people who picked up energy in that particular corner of the room. There is no documentation of a sighting in that area, but she has also felt a strong presence in that spot. She agrees it is a very active hot spot which is paranormal in nature.

I walked around the front of the pool where the diving board is located. I took a base reading of 59degrees. Suddenly I felt a gust of extremely cold air, then a gust of hot air. I broke out into a sweat then I started shivering. I told the psychic and she said this usually happens when the spirit of the little girl is around. She has been sighted in the very spot that I was experiencing temperature changes. I didn't get to see her but I did feel a presence there.

I walked over to a long corridor that was once a dressing room. Some psychics believe this area is a doorway or a portal to another dimension. This is where many spirits can enter our world passing through back and forth. There can be good as well as evil spirits. This is what I was picking up on. I noticed there is a correlation usually when I feel nausea and sick or extremely afraid that I am sensing an evil or possibly a non human presence. I felt very hot and claustrophobic in the dressing room. I could feel a strong presence and got a little scared so I snapped a couple of pictures in the dark and exited out of the area very quickly.

There has been an apparition of an old woman seen diving in the empty pool. She has on an old fashioned bathing suit and swimming cap of the 1950's. I took photos of the area where one of the vortexes is located.

When I viewed the photos, strange streaks of light appeared shooting out of the wall.

The next area we went to was the Engine Room also known as Shaft Alley on Deck G. It seemed very calm there and I didn't sense anything at all. I took some photos near the small stairway but nothing came out in the pictures. There is an area called watertight door number 13. This is a doorway where John Peddler was crushed to death. I photographed this door, but I didn't capture anything unusual.

We walked up a non-moving escalator that led to a theater. This area is usually not part of the tour; but since we were the only two people there, the psychic said we had extra time. She asked us if we wanted to check this area out. Of course we agreed. The psychic said she heard a woman humming near the stage and so did I. At that moment, my friend snapped a picture of the stage and an orb appeared. Other passengers staying on the ship have claimed to have heard a baby crying near the dressing rooms of the theatre.

Another area we explored was the Promenade Deck. I didn't get any anomalies in the pictures that were taken there. However, it did feel very eerie walking through the dimly lit hallways. A smoky, white-film lingered in the air. I felt a scary sensation.

The scariest area of the ship was the Boiler Room on Deck G. We had to walk over a Catwalk on Deck C and then descend downstairs in order to get there. There were some walkways that we had to cross over to explore the decrepit areas. It was very dark and we had to use flashlights in most of the areas. This area is the lowest level of the ship.

As soon as I entered the Boiler Room, I sensed a strong evil presence. It was very dark and cold. We all heard banging sounds in the large room. It felt like someone was watching me as I explored the rooms.

The psychic said she used to communicate with the spirit that resides here. His name is Henry, and he was killed in an explosion in the Boiler Room. She doesn't like to talk to him anymore because of an incident that happened to her. She said one time she was 'channeling' his spirit and he tried to possess her. He entered her body and tried to change her physical appearance. She could feel herself getting taller and wider. She also felt like she was going to start talking in his voice. This is known as transfiguration. Some psychics have this ability. She may not have known she could do this. This is the ability that a psychic allows a spirit to enter their body and alter their psychical appearance. A person can actually see the face of the spirit as they speak through the medium.

In the psychic's case, not only was the face appearing but the actual body of Henry. This was too much for her to take. This was more like possession then transfiguration. Possession is much worse. This is when the spirit inhabits the body and takes total control, never wanting to leave. The psychic was afraid that this would happen to her. Transfiguration is different. This is when the spirit is only there for a short period of time, only to communicate, and then it leaves the body. After this incident, she stopped the communication with him. She seemed genuinely scared and uneasy being in this room. She also appeared to be very nervous and kept looking around. This definitely made me believe that she was telling us the truth.

We decided to explore the back part of the Boiler Room, where she said several people have had alarming experiences. People claimed to have been touched and grabbed in these corridors. There is a back room where some actors stayed during Halloween. They had a small stage set-up for their Ghosts and Legends Show. The actors would stay in this room taking breaks between the shows. They all have heard sounds, voices and seen shadows. It scared them so much that they refused to work or stay there anymore.

The psychic said this is the main area where Henry stays and she didn't want to go there. She stayed behind, alone, in another room. A security guard took us to this area of the Boiler Room. We took a lot of pictures. Orbs appeared in many of the photos in the room where the psychic was standing, and in the areas that we heard the loud banging but not in the back part of the Boiler Room.

When we returned to talk to the psychic she told us that she picked up on Henry's presence. She didn't want to communicate with him so she opened the door and told him to leave. This was around the same time I didn't feel his presence anymore.

When I first went to the back part of the Boiler Room, I sensed his presence, and then it suddenly felt like it was gone. I found out after the incident that this was about the same time the psychic was asking Henry to leave. We were in two different rooms, so I wasn't aware that she did this. The psychic confirmed that she was sensing the same paranormal activity that I was. This made me very happy and excited for someone to finally verify or authenticate what I was experiencing. She said I definitely have some psychic ability and that I am very intuitive. This means I can sense spirits or a presence but I cannot see or hear them. She would first ask me my impressions of certain areas then she would tell me her impressions. They would coincide with each other. She just had a little more detail then I did.

Overall, it was one of the most scary and exciting ghost tours that I have been on. I would love to go back there again and explore the many areas that I didn't get to see the first time. These areas include the kitchen, the orphanage, the morgue, and many long corridors that have reported sightings. The ship is so massive and we were getting tired and running out of time, so we decided to leave. I was very impressed with the evidence that we collected and the personal experiences that we encountered. This was the hi-light of my San Diego vacation.

The Queen Mary Hotel (Orb onstage in theater)
Long Beach, CA. 11/2008

The Queen Mary Hotel
Long Beach, CA 11/2008
(Orb appeared onstage in theatre after we heard a baby crying)

Escalator in the Queen Mary Hotel
Long beach, CA. 11/2008
(Orbs appear hovering here)

The Boiler Room in the Queen Mary Hotel
Long Beach, CA. 11/2008
(The ghost of Henry lingers here – orb in the air)

The Boiler Room in the Queen Mary Hotel
Long Beach, CA. 11/2008
(The ghost of Henry has been sighted here – pinkish orb in the air)

The Swimming Pool Area in the Queen Mary Hotel
Long Beach, CA. 11/2008
(This is the most haunted spot on the ship- three different spirits have been
sighted here and many psychics claim there is a portal located at this spot)
Multiple vortexes surrounding the area.

I hope you have enjoyed the many haunted locations as much as I did. I am currently exploring several haunted sites in New Mexico, Colorado and California. I have been finding many places that contain paranormal activity. I continue to photograph and document my findings. This has been an incredible journey that I hope never ends.

BIBLIOGRAPHY

BOOKS

Adams, Charles J. III. *Coal Country Ghosts Legends and Lore.* Schuylkill and Carbon Counties, Pennsylvania. Exeter House Books, Reading, Pa, 2004 p. 120-141

Adams, Charles J. III. *New York City Ghost Stories.* Exeter House Books, Reading, PA, 1996 p. 86-90

Adams, Charles J. III. *Pocono Ghosts Legends and Lore Book Two.* Exeter House Books, Reading, Pa, 1995 p. 85-87

Belanger, Jeff. *Encyclopedia of Haunted Places.* Franklin Lakes, NJ: New Page Books, 2005 p. 171-172

Branning, Debe. *Sleeping with Ghosts: A Ghost Hunter's Guide to Arizona's Haunted Hotel & Inns.* Phoenix, Arizona, Golden West Publishers, Inc. 2004 p. 47-51, p. 52-55, p. 132-135

Cahill, Robert Ellis. *Haunted Happenings.* Danvers, Massachusetts, Old Saltbox Publishing, 1992 p. 19-30

Cahill, Robert Ellis. *New England's Things That Go Bump in the Night.* Danvers, Massachusetts, Old Saltbox Publishing, 1970 p. 3-5

Cawthorne, Nigel. *Witches-History of a Persecution.* Edison, New Jersey. Chartwell Books, Inc. 2004 p. 13

Lake, Matt, Moran, Scheurman. ***Weird Pennsylvania.*** New York, NY, Sterling Publishing Co. Inc. 2005 p. 168

McManus, Craig. ***The Ghosts of Cape May: Book One.*** Craig McManus, 2005 p. 20-27

Nesbitt, Mark. ***The Ghost Hunters Field Guide- Gettysburg & Beyond.*** Gettysburg, Pa, Second Chance Publications, 2005 p. 27

Polson, Cody. ***Haunted New Mexico- The Ghosts of Albuquerque.*** Baltimore, Publish America, 2004 p. 17- 20 p. 41-46 p. 86-90

Robson, Ellen. ***Haunted Arizona- Ghosts of the Grand Canyon State.*** Phoenix, Arizona, Golden West Publishers, Inc. 2007 p. 34 p. 114 & 119

Svehla, Joe. ***Catch the Spirits- Ghostly Images.*** Gettysburg, Pa, Americana Souvenirs and Gifts, 2005 p. 21-27

Taylor, L.B. Jr. ***The Ghosts of Richmond and nearby environs.*** Progress Printing Co. Inc. 1985 p. 77-81

Wlodarski, Robert James & Anne Powell. ***The Haunted Queen Mary- Long Beach, California.*** West Hills, California, Ghost Publishing, 2000 p. 1-10 p. 16, 18, 20, 21, 26, 27 & 49

BIBLIOGRAPHY

WEBSITES

"Albuquerque Attraction, Albuquerque Travel, New Mexico Sightseeing."
Http:// www.bottger.com/old-town-hidden-gems.htm

"Bring down The Tom Quick Monument Petition."
Http://www.petitiononline.com/4truth/petition.html

"Burying Point". Http://www.graveaddiction.com/burypt.html

"The Callaghan-Kays Tragedy."
Http://www.catskillarchive.com/rrextra/ertrag.html

"Checking Your 6th Sense-Succeed Through Using Your Senses: School for Champions."
Http. //www.school-forchampions.com/sense/6thcheck.htm

"Cinema Treasures - Milford Theatre."
Http://cinematreasures.org/theater/10238

"Dead of Night Tours of Plymouth Massachusetts. Nightly Lantern Tours, Ghost photos."
Http:// www.deadofnightghosttours.com/burial.htm

"Divining Rod." Http://en.wikipedia.org/wiki/Divining-_rod

"Ectoplasm." Http://skepdic.com/ectoplasm.html

"The Flamingo Hilton."
Http://www.ghostinmysuitcase.com/places/flamingo/index.htm

"Gaslamp Quarter."
Http://www.gaslampquarter.org/history/thehouse.php

"Ghosts and Ectoplasm."
Http.//inin.essortment.com/whatisectoplas_rkki.htm

"Ghost hunt of Rancho de Corrales Restaurant."
Http://www.sgha.net/corrales/rdc.html

"A Ghost Story."
Http://www.double-eagle-mesilla.com/ghost-story.htm

"Ghost Hunters of the West Plains."
Http://community-2.webtv.net/ghostpic/GHOSTSANDSPIRITS

"Haunted Hotels Las Vegas, NV."
Http://www.hoteltravelcheck.com/haunted-hotels-las-vegas.html

"Haunted Museum Club in Flagstaff Arizona."
Http://www.legendsofamerica.com/Az-Museumclub.html

"History of Salem Massachusetts Ma Genealogy Ancestry Ancestors
Salem Cemeteries."
Http://www.gravematter.com/cem-ma-salem.Asp

"The House of Seven Gables."
Http://www.graveaddiction.com/sevengab.html

"Hunting Liberace's Ghost."
Http://men.style.com/details/features/full?id=content_286

"Jim Thorpe, Pennsylvania-Old Jail Museum."
Http://www.roadsideamerica.com/tips/getAttraction.
php3?tip_AttractionNo==6815

"Learning to Channel the Energy."
Http://www.chioshealing.com/HealingLevel1/ChannelEnergy/
channelenergy.htm

"Lenni Lenape Indian Tribe (Delaware Indians, Lenapes."
Http://www.geocities.com/bigorrin/lenape_kids.htm

"Liberace-Bio-History of Gay & Lesbian Life, Milwaukee WI-People."
Http://www.mkelgbthist.org/people/peo-1/liberace.htm

"Ouija Boards." Http://www.casleodspirits.com/ouijaboards.html

"The Plaza n Mesilla New Mexico."
Http://www.oldmesilla.org/html/the_plaza.htm

"The Queen Mary of Longbeach-History and Hauntings."
http://www.legendsofamerica.com/CA-QueenMary.html

"Rain Dance." Http://www.indians.org/articles/rain-dance.html

"Rain Dance."
Http://www.native-languages.org/composition/rain-dance.html

"Real Magick Article": "Divining Rods." by Sherry Sims"
Http://realmagick.com/articles/93/993.htm

"The Red Lion Inn."
Http://www.historictraveler.com/primedia/Red-lion.adp

"Salem Massachusetts- Salem Tales."
Http://salemweb.com/tales/charter.shtml

"Salem Witch Trials Memorial."
Http://www.salemweb.com/memorial/stonesintro.shtml

"Spooked! Queer Paranormal Road Trip: Carluccio's Tivoli Gardens."
Http://moonspenders.blogspot.com/2008/05/queer-paranor-mal-road-trip-carluccios.html

"Tom Quick – Indian Slayer."– Schoonmaker
Http://www.jrbookonline.com/HTML_docs/tom_quick_schoonmaker.htm

"The Underground Railroad."
Http://www.freedomcenter.org/underground-railroad

"Virginia History." Http://www.virginia.com

"What is Ectoplasm." Http://ghostwatchers.org/ectoplasm.html

"William Heath Davis house in San Diego, California."
Http://gothere.com/sandiego/Ghosts/DavisHouse/default.htm

"The World Famous Whaley House."
Http://www.whaleyhouse.org

www.ingramcontent.com/pod-product-compliance
Lightning Source LLC
Chambersburg PA
CBHW030253290526
45785CB00001B/66